MARKET ECONOMY

&

POLICY ON TWO

DOMESTIC CURRENCIES

A new solution group for macroeconomic stability and economic crisis prevention

DO DUC LUONG

Market Economy & Policy On Two Domestic Currencies

Copyright © 2009 DO DUC LUONG

All rights reserved.

ISBN:1495232913
ISBN-13: 978-1495232916

Market Economy & Policy On Two Domestic Currencies

Vietnamese document is published by National Economics University Publishing House, Hanoi in March 2009. English document is translated by Hanoi Foreign Languages Education and Translation Co., Ltd.

Market Economy & Policy On Two Domestic Currencies

CONTENTS

Introduction

1. MARKET ECONOMY   Pg 7

2. KNOTS IN THE ECONOMY   Pg 62

3. MACROECONOMIC REGULATION   Pg 97

4. POLICY ON TWO DOMESTIC CURRENCIES   Pg 136

Introduction

Hanoi, January 2009

The entire world has just said good-bye to the year of 2008 with a heavy mood. Everyone welcomes the new spring with decisions of tightening expenditure to deal with the economic crisis evaluated as the biggest crisis since the industrial big slump in 1930s of last century. In 2008 securities index in our country reduced over 60% and average reduction in the world was 40%. Low economic yield and unemployment increase are popular situation in all countries, so the governments must issue the huge demand stimulating packages to save the economy. This economic crisis can last until 2010 and cause serious damage to many countries in the world.

The surprised thing for everyone is that the crisis happened quickly and strongly, but at the beginning of the year 2008 nobody received any official warning on the economic crisis, only a credit crisis rising from substandard lending in America. In the middle of the year 2008 we were known about a global financial crisis happening and in the last months of the year 2008 everyone was witness of a global economic crisis at serious level. Was the theoretical models in economics backward than the reality? Or at least they had many big gaps and macroeconomic analysis became indefinite. Therefore, economists must spend much time and effort to make the subject of economics become the scientific subject which grasps every movement of the economy. So, any new creation of professional researches or amateur researches in the field of economics has high referent value and event character.

In this book, besides the contents with general features on economics, each chapter mentions to remarkable new matters at micro *level and macro level of market economy. In chapter 1, we can find a method of defining the commodity value according to a new logic; in chapter 2, you have reason to worry about a economic model without progress; in chapter 3, we make acquaintance of general macroeconomic index and two solutions of regulating the economy; in chapter 4 – the final chapter – this chapter can make a strong impression on readers by a proposal on the currency policy without antecedent in the reality. Moreover, through this book, some important concepts in the economics described briefly and concisely help readers easy to approach.*

Because this book contains many innovated opinions, the content of the book can be surrounded by controversy or query in different groups of readers. You can send email to the writer to contribute your ideas about the content of the book or share your opinion. E-mail for contact: do.duc.luong.vn@gmail.com

Writer: **Do Duc Luong**

Chapter 1
MARKET ECONOMY

In the old days, under the primitive commune regime, people lived in small communities called Clan or Tribe. They lived and worked together under gregarious form. With the rudimental production tools, the yield from cultivation, breeding and hunting are only enough for use in the community and have no redundant products. The situation of enough food, enough money was popular in all communes. That was the typical self-sufficiency economic model in the human society. In the later, in the advanced economic-social forms, we still find the features of self-sufficiency model existing in backward economic area.

With the time, creative labor changed production tools, labor productivity was improved with requirement of raising the professional skills. Since that division of labor and production specialization appeared, marking a big change of production force. Groups of people in the society made different products to satisfy their demand and exchange to maximize the utility level. Commodity economy appeared naturally as the indispensable request of the life.

1.1 Currency

The simple commodity economy according to the type of exchanging goods operates fluently only when number of kinds of commodity can count by figures. In reality, the production is not monotonous like this, the increasingly commodity quantity bothers the process of exchange. Clothes producer who has redundant products and wants to exchange the food must find the breeder who has demand of using clothes, it is not easy. Using the intermediate goods – a beginning currency form – as parity exchange product is very useful in the commodity economy in the transition stage from simply to complex. Suppose the society agrees to consider rice as intermediate commodity in the exchange process and used everywhere, whenever in the community, then the exchange problem of producers becomes easier. Clothes producer who has redundant products and wants to exchange the food is not necessary to find the breeder who needs clothes, they can exchange clothes for rice of somebody and then exchange rice for food of any breeder. This new exchange method, executing two steps but two simple steps, is like as changing a complicated problem into two simple problems.

Currency is an intermediate commodity (sheep, cloth...) or a special designed product (paper money, polymer money ...) which is established as a convention by the society as a value measurer for every other commodity and service during the process of transaction between buyers and sellers.

At the beginning stage of the commodity economy, currency is often an intermediate familiar commodity as sheep, cloth or even salt. In the later, mining industry develops, people use the metal money with more preeminent features than kinds of currency as commodity. Nowadays, paper money, polymer money and metal money are popular forms of currency used by countries. These currency kinds are not commodity, but a special product form based on the sophisticated print technology and unique production skills.

Commodities and services will be used by the people or be the input for the production process, however, currency is only intermediate exchange item and it doesn't lose during the circulation process. The currency is used as payment mean and it is accounting unit in the whole economy. Because of strict management by the Government, currency has stable value and people use it as the mean of hoarding, saving according to the time.

1.2 Market

The commodity economy takes place the mutual exchange between buyers and sellers on the same commodity. In the first stage of commodity exchange, seller and seller are individuals, have no relation. The exchange process takes place spontaneously or dictated by feeling. In many cases, the price of a kind of commodity is different between this group and other group although they live nearly. The commodity circulation develops increasingly, makes sellers and buyers close to each other. Sellers discuss together on the situation of commodity supply, product quality and the price. Buyers exploit their information and from commodity suppliers. Since that, the commodity price is formed according to general platform with the popular features and commocity volume for exchange. The appearance of commodity market creates good conditions for exchange activity based on the clear informat on and sound competition between buyers and sellers.

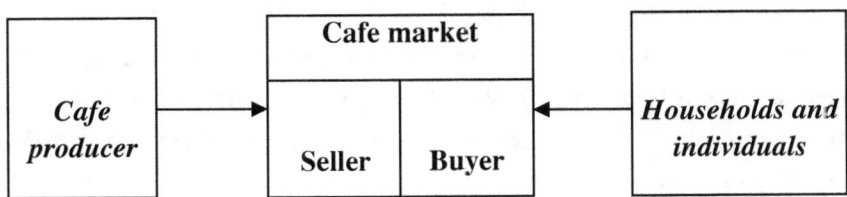

Figure 1.1: Cafe market

The market is a form of "shapeless economic organization" created by the interlacing relations between seller and buyer, since that determine the price of commodity (services), commodity quantity for supply and payment method among parties.

We know that, enterprise, cooperative, supermarket or market are "shaped economic organizations". There, there is the management system, fixed address and even juridical personality. The market is not clear. The market is only "slack alliance" between seller and buyer of the same kinds of goods. When we mentions to Cafe market, we want to mention to the set of suppliers and customers who have the demand on buying and selling cafe. Among them, there are lots of relations of exchanging information to establish the temporary equilibrium on the price, yield for exchange. There are many kinds of markets such as: rice market, fruits and vegetables market, real estate market, securities market... The market scale is diversified such as: local market, regional market, domestic market, international market.

1.3 Market economy

The market economy is the high-grade commodity economy. The development process from the simple economy to the market economy must spend another intermediate stage hereof called temporarily as concentrated commodity economy. In the concentrated commodity economy, commodity exchange doesn't bring spontaneous character, but concentrate into commodity market in local areas and have no connection among resident areas, so it can't consider as markets.

The market economy is the economic model which commodity (service) markets operate freely, through that enterprises decide by them the plan of business operation, households select the suitable spending methods.

Commodity markets make "the front" of the economy, and behind are many enterprises with fierce competitive strategies to exist and develop. Behind that "front" millions of households with limited income must calculate the expenditure plan so that it is economical and effective.

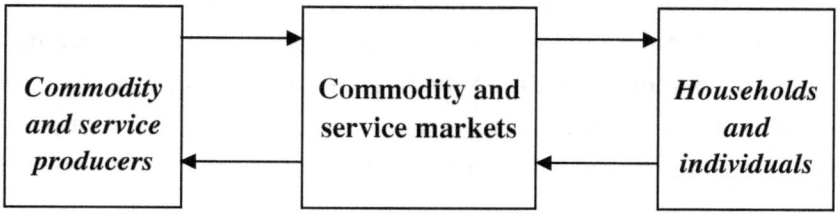

Figure 1.2: Relation between production and consumption through market

The enterprises supply output goods products to the market but purchase the materials and input production tools from the market. They select the manpower from labor market and borrow capital from the monetary market. Households buy commodities and services for consumption in the markets; concurrently supply the labor service and idle capital resource to the market.

The commodity market operating freely means it is operated according to natural rules without imposition by the Government. Forbidding commerce is not suitable for free market. However, competent authorities inspect the market to prevent the counterfeit, imitation... this is necessary and benefit for the market. With some special commodity markets such as medicine, veterinary drug... the business condition is not easy as other common commodity markets. Tax policy of the Government deforms the market bigger or smaller but doesn't change the common rules of the market. Intervention of the Government into the market with method of both managing and creating good condition so that the market develop healthily takes place popularly in the world, different only from intervention level.

In opposition to the market economy model is centrally planned economy. The economic model in which the state controls every activity from production, distribution to consumption has ever existed in the system of socialist states before. This imperative economy overloads for state authorities and doesn't create the competitive motive force in enterprises as well as laborers. The result is low labor productivity, resources waste, non-high product quality and finally the economy based on administrative subsidies collapses.

1.4 Equation of exchange equilibrium

In this section, we establish an equation on binding relation between commodity and currency in the circulation process. This is not a new proposal, in reality the equation of commodity exchange equilibrium was discovered for a long time by economists, however, in majority of documents on economics circulating, this matter is not explained in details so readers are hard to imagine. Here we need to study more detailed. Simply, we have an example on a brief economic model in which only three groups of people produce closely and exchange goods to each other. Three items for buying and selling are food, foodstuff and clothes with quantity and unit price as below:

Commodity	Volume	Unit price	Turnover
Food	900 kg	10,000 dong	9,000,000 dong
Foodstuff	90 kg	50,000 dong	4,500,000 dong
Clothes	10 sets	100,000 dong	1,000,000 dong

The process of buying, selling, exchanging commodity among three groups of people is divided into many times; each trading order has small volume but taking place continuously in a year. The first group sells the food and uses money earned to buy foodstuff and clothes; the second group sells the foodstuff and buys food and clothes; the third group sells clothes and buys food and foodstuff. We call M cash mount issued to serve the process of circulating goods, so M is total cash held by three groups for trading. In this model, suppose that M = 1,000,000 dong (One million dong).

From above data table, we are easy to calculate total commodity transaction turnover in the year as 14,500,000 dong. We find that three groups of people use only cash amount 1,000,000 dong but re-circulating many times and in a year having total trading turnover as 14,500,000 dong. If call V currency circulating speed, MV = 14,500,000, infer V = 14.5. It means within 1 year, they re-circulate the current money amount average 14.5 times to execute successfully transaction value 14,500,000 dong.

Now, from above simple example, we generalize for a real economy with tens thousand kinds of commodity, service put into circulation and trading activities take place continuously. Commodity from production place to consumers must spend many intermediate stages such as distributor, general agent, and retail store. In each intermediate stage, commodity are changed the owner, the price is defined and money is handed. Because commodity must circulate through many intermediate stages, total transaction commodity volume in the economy is greater than total commodity volume produced. A transaction having commodity and currency exchange is called a successful transaction. Selling commodity on credit or consigning products aren't considered as a successful transaction, when currency is paid by buyer, we have a successful transaction.

If call Q_i and P_i in turn volume and unit price of i-th successful transaction, call n total number of times of successful transaction during the examined period. We have:

Turnover of i-th successful transaction: $Q_i \times P_i$

Total transaction turnover during the examined period:

$$\sum Q_i \times P_i \ (i = 1...n)$$

Call M total issued currency value, V average circulation times of currency during the examined period, we have following equation:

$$\sum Q_i P_i = MV \quad (1)$$

This is the equation of commodity - currency exchange equilibrium in the market economy.

Total transaction turnover of commodity and service in a defined duration is equal to product of currency volume and average circulation speed of currency.

Next we change equation (1) to shorter form.

Call Q total volume of transaction commodity and service: $Q = \sum Q_i$

Set $P = \dfrac{\sum Q_i P_i}{Q}$, P is called general average price of all commodities and services. So, $PQ = \sum Q_i P_i$ \hfill (2)

Finally from (1) and (2) we have the shorten equation as following:

$$PQ = MV \qquad (3)$$

In which:

Q is total unit of commodity and service for executing the transaction

P is general average price of all commodities and services

M is total circulating currency value

V is average circulating times of currency

Now try applying equation (3) in the example on simple economic model mentioned above to calculate all its values.

PQ = MV = 14,500,000, with M = 1,000,000 → V = 14.5

$Q = \sum Q_i$, so, Q = 900 + 90 + 10 = 1000 →

P = 14,500,000/1000 = 14,500

From the equation PQ = MV we have following formulas: $P = \dfrac{MV}{Q}$ and $M = \dfrac{PQ}{V}$. These formulas have important meaning in analyzing the inflation and currency policy which we will mention in next chapters.

From theory to reality

In the reality, volume of commodities and services is very big, concurrently each kind of commodity circulates through many different intermediate stages, so synthesizing all transactions of whole economy is unfeasible and overlaps. To simplify, people often total up the final yield of commodities and services of the economy to put in application and analysis in equation of exchange equilibrium.

If call Q value of final yield of commodities and services converted according to the price level of time as original point; call P index of current average price compared with the original time; call M total average circulation currency value; call V basic currency circulation speed, we have the equation: PQ = MV.

1.5 Business operation expenses, revenue and profit

Commodity production is an important stage of the economy, executed by business households, cooperatives or companies; hereafter we call enterprises in general. Enterprises use combining the input factors to change into commodity products at output.

Figure 1.3: Input and output of production process

On ownership, the enterprise can belong to private ownership, collective ownership or state owned. A typical enterprise includes board of directors, management apparatus and investment capital. Enterprise board of directors includes representatives of enterprise owner; they plan the business strategy; establish the management apparatus and take part in controlling the activities of the enterprise. Management apparatus includes people who are dynamic, have ability of management and professional knowledge; they decide the production plan, method of product consumption, manpower recruitment and salary regulation in the enterprise. Investment capital (owning or borrowing) is divided into two parts: fixed capital and circulating capital. Fixed capital includes land, factory, machines, equipment and transport vehicle. Circulating capital includes cash, production raw materials, semi-finished product and inventory.

Input factors can divided into three sections. The first section includes raw materials or semi-finished products put into the production, and then they are combined together and changed into commodity products at output. The second section includes resource of fuel, electrical energy for operating machines, equipment and transport vehicle. The third section, very important, includes manpower, technicians; they are people who operate equipment, pack products and transport commodity to consume.

The output of production process includes commodity products with plentiful designs and models. That is the crystallization between the creative labor of human and the diversity of raw material resource in the nature. Each commodity product has private use to satisfy some demand of people.

1.5.1 Business operation expenses

Business operation expenses are all expenses during the business operation process from stage of importing the input raw materials to stage of packing the finished products and delivering. It includes expenses of raw materials, energy, worker salary, fixed assets depreciation;... management expense, capital borrowing expense and tax expense. In brief, there are many kinds of expense. However, to simplify the problem and give advantage to research, we divide the business operation expenses into three kinds of expense: manpower expense, material resources expense and derived expense.

Manpower expenses are expenses related to human factor in the process of production and distribution of products; including salary, bonus for staff and enterprise management apparatus, shift meal expense, health insurance expense, labor safety expense. Another important component in manpower expense is expense for training, improving professional knowledge for staff and investment expense for researching and developing new products.

Material resources expenses are expenses related to physical factors during the process of production; including expenses of raw materials, energy, design and packing of products, fixed assets depreciation, expense of repairing machines, equipment, extinguish system, environmental protection.

Derived expenses are expenses related indirectly to the process of business operation; including financial expense (if any), tax and fee, trademark protection, intellectual property registration, commercial copyright, and especially marketing advertisement expense.

If call business operation expense P_{sx-kd}, manpower expense P_n, material resources expense P_v and derived expense P_p, we have following formula:

$$P_{sx-kd} = P_n + P_v + P_p \qquad (1)$$

Beside the way of dividing total business operation expenses into three groups of expense as above, we can divide in other way, for example, into four groups including: production expense, sales expense, enterprise management expense and financial expense.

Production expenses include expenses related to the stage of production of the enterprise such as: expense of raw material, energy, product packing; assets depreciation; manpower expense...

Sales expenses include the marketing advertisement expense, delivery expense, tax and fee...

Enterprise management expenses include the expense of operating the management apparatus and administrative units, insurance expense, labor safety expense, expense for training, improving professional knowledge for staff and investment expense for researching and developing new products...

Financial expenses include expenses related to borrowing capital, renting financial assets ...

If designate production expense as P_{sx}, sales expense as P_{bh}, enterprise management expense as P_{ql}, financial expense as P_{tc}, we have:

$$P_{sx-kd} = P_{sx} + P_{bh} + P_{ql} + P_{tc}$$

In reality, many enterprises operate in many fields, besides the main business activity, they take part in the financial investment and other investment operations. Here we calculate only business operation expense related to main business activity of the enterprise.

Enterprises produce not only one kind of commodity or service but also diversifications of product. Then if we want to calculate the business operation expense of each item, we calculate three kinds of particular expense for each item and then add together according to the formula (1).

1.5.2 Revenue

Revenue is total sales turnover of the enterprise in a defined duration. If designate D as revenue, P as average commodity price, Q as consumption commodity yield, we have:

$$D = PQ \qquad (2)$$

After selling, manufacturer bears responsibility for product warranty in a certain period and can spend an expense amount for warranty and maintenance. So, real revenue is the difference between net revenue and revenue deduction.

If the enterprise sells many commodity items, the revenue of each kind of commodity can be calculated according to the formula (2), in which the price and quantity is correlative to each kind.

Similar to the section of calculating the production expense, here we calculate only revenue related to main business activity of the enterprise without paying attention to kinds of revenue collected from other investment activities.

1.5.3 Profit

The profit of the enterprise is the difference between the revenue and the business operation expense in a period. Because the business operation expense as above includes taxes as well as the enterprise reward funds, the profit in this section is net profit – the final profit of investor or shareholders. If designate M as profit, from above result we have:

$$M = D - P_{sx-kd}$$

There are three cases happening to value of M correlative to three levels of effective operation of the enterprise. If M = 0, it means the revenue is equal to the business operation expense, the enterprise breaks even. If M > 0, the revenue is bigger than the expense, we say the enterprise is profitable. If M < 0, the revenue is smaller than the expense, the enterprise is unprofitable.

After calculating the profit of the enterprise, we have not evaluated the effect of the investment. Suppose that two enterprises have the same absolute profit M, however the first enterprise has scale of capital, worker quantity doubling to the second enterprise, we find that the first enterprise has the business effect lower than the second enterprise. So, to evaluate the effect of the investment capital, we must calculate the rate of return of the enterprise. This value is defined by the way: dividing the profit in a year of the enterprise by equity and then converting according to percent rate. The equity of the enterprise is not always equal to total investment capital of the enterprise because total investment capital can include borrowing capital.

The inflation reduces the purchasing power of the currency, so the price of assets invested before of the enterprise is changed now. Therefore, the equity of the enterprise must be calculated according to current price, then evaluating the rate of return has the real meaning. Like this, compare of business effect among enterprises will ensure the accuracy. From now, when mention to the investment capital of the enterprise, it means we mention to the equity of the enterprise adjusted according to current price.

If call R the rate of return of the enterprise, I the equity of the enterprise, M the profit in a year; we have:

$$R = \frac{M}{I} \times 100\%$$

R is positive when M > 0; R = 0 when M = 0; R is negative when M < 0.

If define the profit and the particular investment capital for business operation of each kind of commodity, we can calculate the rate of return for each item.

We note that, here we calculate only the profit related to main business activity.

1.6 Selection of consumers

Each individual or household has an expenditure budget according to the plan, subject to rich level and private hobbies; they have the expenditure selections according to private style. In general, first priority is for the expenditure serving the essential demand such as food, house service, clothes, study, travel and healthcare. Next is buying or replacing household appliances such as television, fridge, computer,… and demand of entertainment to improve the spirit life. People who have high income often go to restaurant, hotel, beauty salon, buy car, use high-grade tourist service… or live in expensive villa.

Beside expenditure budget, a typical household has a list of assets including one or many kinds such as real estate, bond, bank deposit…, precious metals, stock.

The expenditure budget of families is supplemented from monthly personal income of members in the family. Income items through the investment or assets liquidation can be added to family expenditure budget. Many families, not all, at some time use the borrowing money to add to expenditure budget.

With a budget limited and expenditure plan defined before, individuals and households select in the market to find the items having the suitable price and quality to get the max utility. For example, poor households with tight expenditure budget, when they select the commodity, they can't pay attention to the quality, they must be interested in the price. With rich households, the commodity quality is the first priority, after that it is the price.

Consumption belief in people increases, or in other words, families are ready to loosen the purse-strings when the social economic condition is stable, the job is enough. With each household, when the income increases - the expenditure increases, when the income decreases - the expenditure decreases. With households owning the list of assets, the change of assets value in the market affects to the consumption psychology. Suppose that price of stock increases stably and at high level, the value of stock assets booms, stock investors earn big money and they will be more open-handed in expenditure and shopping. When the periodical statistics show that the economy is in the recession, unemployment, households will response by contraction, retrenchment to prevent the risks whenever.

1.7 Currency interest rate and average rate of return in business operation

We find that, the poverty still exists around the world. However, the global population increases continuously. In almost countries, the situation is similar. Meanwhile the natural resources are more and more scarce. A basic contradiction in the economy is the demand of human is higher and higher, but supply ability is limited. That contradiction pushes the material price to increase and it is the cause of price inflation.

1.7.1 Currency interest rate

The reality shows that, forming a credit market is because of objective reasons. The families understand that, the currency is also a mean for hoarding the value. So, with total monthly income, they add only a part into regular expenditure budget, and a part is hoarded for important intentions later or preventing the risks. Some enterprises trade profitably, but they don't divided all the profit into shareholders, they gather money to execute the investment project in the future. In another aspect, many households have demand of buying house or car and they hoarded nearly all amount of money for shopping, because the necessary demand they want to buy but not enough money. Many enterprises trading profitably are short of capital to expand the scale, increase the competitive ability and earn more profit. Demand and supply will create the market. Nowadays, the commercial bank system is the center of the credit market in each country. The banks mobilize the idle balances in the society according to different schedules and then lend the potential customers.

If the money is stored in the cabinet or strong-box of the family, in the later the amount is the same, no change. However, the money is to lend, it makes the interest, the longer the time for lending is, the bigger the interest is. This is because of at least two reasons. Firstly, although lending friends or depositing at a bank, lending still contains a certain implicit risk because the partner is loss-marking or goes bankrupt leading to incapacity for payment, so the interest rate is the reward for acceptance of risk. Secondly, the inflation decreases the purchasing power of currency according to the time, so the interest rate is the compensation for depositor to balance the purchasing power at two times. The depositor is enjoyed the saving interest from borrower through the intermediate role of the bank.

If you have the temporary idle balances and don't have demand of investing hazardously, apart from depositing, some other investment products in the financial market make you pay attention such as: Treasury bill, public bond, corporate bond. This is the financial instruments issued by the Government or companies with different dead-line and the interest rate level defined before.

1.7.2 Average rate of return in business operation

Depositing or buying the bond is the simple and safe investment form, contributing capital into business operation or investing in stock contains many risks. Business operation enterprises have many relations in the operation process.

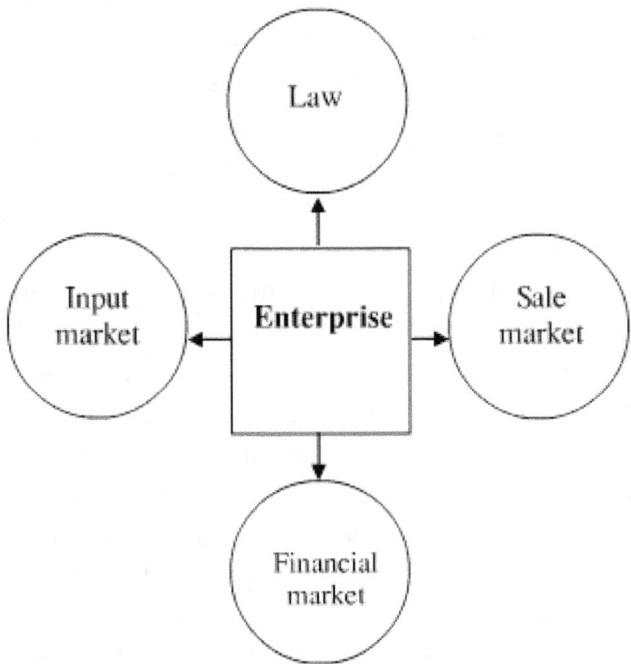

Figure 1.4: Main relations of the enterprise

Firstly, the enterprises must produce, trade according to the regulation of the law, execute the current tax policy. With the time, the law system is continuously completed and has the changes affecting strongly the business operation of the enterprise. The financial market has a strong attachment to the enterprise through services of mobilizing capital, investment trust and multilateral payments operations. Currency interest rate, exchange rates, and the liquidity in the interbank market are the matters cared by the enterprises. The market of the input factors is the place where the enterprise imports the materials, sells the finished products, energy and recruits manpower serving to business operations. The sale market of output commodity of the enterprises can be in the country or abroad, the relationship between the manufacturer and sale market is very important and has permanence in each enterprise. In the background of globalization, the investment capital flows circulate quickly and the commercial relation develops, the commodity markets change strongly, create many risks and squeeze on competition for the enterprises.

Consider the relation between the enterprise and the rest of economy to show the complicated level of business operation. The reasons which create the instability in the market of finance – currency, the shocks in the market of commodities, services, technology changing too fast or the unstable legal environment can create the irresistible risks for the enterprises. In the first months of the year 2008, the inflation in our country increased quickly, the state bank executed the solution of tightening the currency, pushed the lending interest rate too high, the small and medium enterprises hardly approached to borrowing resources leading to the stagnant business operation, many enterprises produced half-heartedly or forced to bankrupt. In the middle of the year 2008, the price of many important input commodities such as petrol, metal ore, food... doubled than that at the beginning of the year, and then suddenly halved, even had one-third left at the end of the year, this shocked to many enterprises. The financial crisis in 2008 originated from United State and spread around the world, now as the world economic crisis is a big storm. In United State, the Government of this country spends fearlessly one thousand billion USD to rescue the insurance groups, complexes of lending money on mortgage or bank financial institutions before the risk of falling. Besides that many great names in US finance must incorporate or go bankrupt. In addition, "VIPs" in US automobile manufacture branch are appealing to the support from the Government to avoid the line collapse.

Know the risks enclosing to business operation, the enterprises want the suitable profit to balance the investment effect. The rate of return of the enterprise in general must be higher than the input interest rate at banks to attract the investment. We know that individuals or community who provides capital to trade is because of the basic target: profit. There are charitable organizations, they establish the business units to create the jobs for street children or somebody establishes company to create the reputation. Cases like this are insignificant. Some people don't like to be in somebody's employ, they establish the small business to work by themselves, their goal is also profit, but if failing they accept considering their effort as interest. An important question is: How much profit do the enterprises want and how is average profit in reality? For the enterprises, the profit is as much as possible; they always use every chance to increase the income. However, the business world is very fierce, there are winner and loser, there are success and failure. With entire economy in general, most of enterprises get the suitable rate of return.

General model on market economy

We consider the general economic model in figure 1.5 including fully components in pure competitive background to establish the short-term balance of the economy. This model supposes that the economy is close, pure competitive and the policies of financial year - currency is stable.

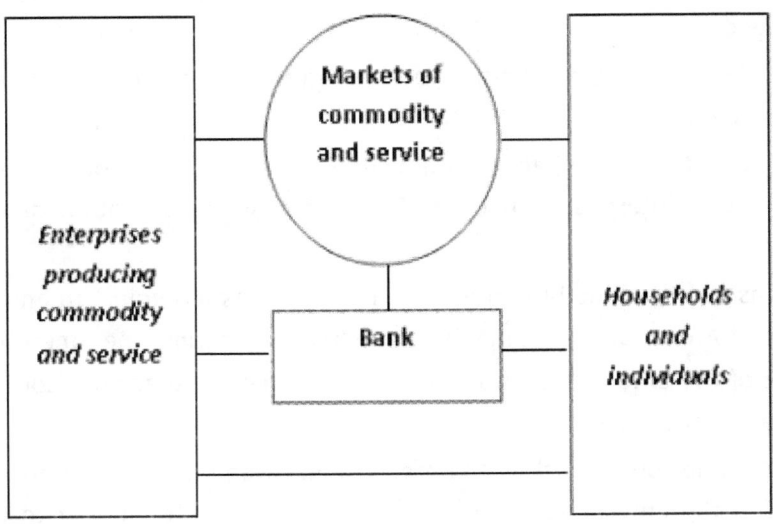

Figure 1.5: General model on market economy

The enterprises provide commodity to the market and receive the input commodity in the market including raw materials, semi-products, energy and labor service. The banks provide the credit to the enterprises but receive the investment trust and interbank payment operation. Households and individuals buy consumer goods in the markets concurrently provide the labor service to the market. Households have demand of depositing, borrowing capital and paying by the bank. Households also supply manpower, direct investment capital to the enterprises and enjoy the income and revenue.

Average rate of return of enterprises block

The enterprises desire the high profit; they must find the way of increasing the revenue and decreasing the input expenses. However, households with limited budget want to buy goods with cheap price and the salary of members of the family is as high as possible. At first sight, we think that is the severe contradiction, but in the fact, it is easy to harmonize because the benefit of two parties is close for the goal of existing and developing together. Markets of commodity – service and manpower salary balance automatically and operate fluently as arranged.

If designate R_{DN} as average rate of return of enterprise block in a certain period.

Z as total of companies, production units, business households… (Called the enterprises) in every fields of business operation of the economy.

I_i as equity of the i-th enterprise, (i = 1...Z). As foregoing, to ensure the uniformity and reasonableness when comparing the operation effect of the enterprises, this value must be calculated again according to the current price.

M_i as net profit of the i-th enterprise in a year. So, if we know the profit of the enterprise in any period of time, need to convert to the profit calculated in a year.

R_i as rate of return of the i-th enterprise in a certain period of time;

$$R_i = \frac{M_i}{I_i} \times 100\%.$$

We have: $R_{DN} = \dfrac{R_1 I_1 + R_2 I_2 + \ldots + R_z I_z}{I_1 + I_2 + \ldots + I_z} = \dfrac{\sum R_i I_i}{\sum I_i} = \dfrac{\sum M_i}{\sum I_i} \times 100\%$

The average rate of return of all the enterprises is equal to the rate of return calculated commonly for entire of business block.

Because the currency interest rate changes according to short-term time with the situation of price inflation, subject to each period of economic development, the absolute value of R_{DN} don't reflect exactly the operation effect of business block.

If we call R_{tb} arithmetic average of the interest rate of input and output of the bank system in a certain stage; R_{DN} as average rate of return of business block in same stage; and put $\Delta R = R_{DN} - R_{tb}$; then ΔR is the value showing better on the level of effective operation of business block when comparing with savings interest rate level in same stage. When average rate of return R_{DN} is more than average interest rate R_{tb}, we have $\Delta R > 0$; when $R_{DN} = R_{tb}$, we have $\Delta R = 0$; when $R_{DN} < R_{tb}$ we have $\Delta R < 0$.

Now we start to go into the core and interesting matter of this item that is to find the answer of the question on average rate of return of the enterprises. To have the relative exact answer, we have to survey a business cycle with hot and cold states of the economy. Through each development stage in the economic cycle, basic factors such as: price of commodity, currency interest rate, psychographics and investment change; this affects definitely to production scale and operation effect of the enterprises. Notice that the economic model considered in this section is the close economy, perfect competition and having little intervention of the Government.

We start the prosperous development stage of the economy. Then the inflation is at average level, suitable interest rate, moderate unemployment and high economic yield. This temporary equilibrium state is called **hot equilibrium state** of the economy, consumption belief and investment is at high level. Commodity price trends increasingly meanwhile the salary and interest rate increase more slowly, so average rate of return of the enterprises is greater than the lending interest rate of banks. At that time, the enterprises want to borrow more money to expand the business operation to get more profit. The investment capital in entire economy increases uniformly, enough job, the income of households is improved, expenditure in the society increases. In the stage of prosperous economy, the inflation and the interest rate increase, the unemployment decreases, the economic yield is always at high level. *This stage is shown by section 0-1 in figure 1.6.*

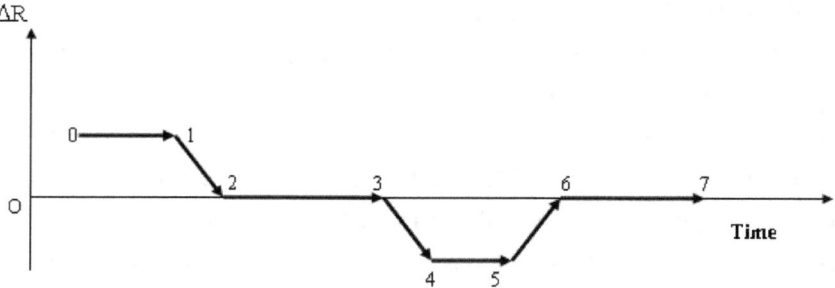

Figure 1.6: The relative change of average rate of return of business block comparing with banking interest rate (ΔR) through different development stages of economic cycle

The commodity price increases continuously with the time and at some time, the inflation rate is higher than saving interest rate. Many people want to keep money to look up the working chance and not want to deposit money into the bank because the current interest rate is not attractive. To ensure liquidity and keep the customers, banks concurrently increase saving interest rate and lending interest rate. High inflation leads to decrease real income of employees and pressure for increasing salary in the enterprises. High capital expense and pressure of increasing salary make the enterprises limit the investment. At this time, average rate of return of the enterprises starts to trend going down. *This stage is shown by section 1-2 in figure 1.6.*

Investment capital in business operation increases strongly in the previous stage, now produces the products and make increasing the output commodity yield, in which quantity of consumption commodity for supply also increases. Because of high interest rate, households economize more and decrease expenditure, so demand of consumption commodity decreases, leading to that consumption commodity price trends to decrease. The enterprises which produce consumption commodity will decrease the profit and limit the expanse of production. The dull situation in the enterprises which produce consumption commodity will spread quickly to area of the enterprises which produce raw materials and tools. Therefore, the common investment tendency in whole economy is temporarily slack. At that time, average rate of return of the enterprises is lower than domestic lending interest rate, but better than the input interest rate of the bank. Average rate of return of the enterprises is like this, however when consider each particular enterprise, it is different. Some enterprises get the rate of return higher than the lending interest rate level of the bank, and they want to borrow more capital to expand the business. The enterprises which get the rate of return lower than the lending interest rate level of the bank, but higher than the interest rate of saving deposit trend to stabilize the production, not expanding the scale but not want to narrow the production. The enterprises which have the rate of return lower than saving deposit interest rate or do at a loss find the way of narrow the production or dissolve. So, three groups of enterprise which have the different business effect, select the private direction and general production scale of the economy change at small level. At this equilibrium state, the situation of business operation and commodity price in the markets starts to stabilize, the bank interest rate is suitable, and expenditure activities of families equilibrate to supply commodity resource. We call this is **stable equilibrium state** of the economy. *This* *stage is shown by section 2-3 in figure 1.6.*

Now we continue to suppose that while the economy is at stable equilibrium state, there is a shock on the market of real estate. The script can follow: Because in previous years, people who have demand of buying the house increase, the real estate companies mobilize the big capital resource to invest in this lucrative field. The speculators also enter in the market to find the short-term profit, so appear imaginary demand everywhere. Because want to earn more profit, the real estate companies concentrate in building the high-grade apartments and villas to sell. When the projects complete, the investors understand that, the real demand on villas and high-grade apartments is very low, mainly the speculation activity of creating the imaginary demand. The real estate market freezes temporarily, the price reduces strongly, projects under construction stop temporarily, the workers in construction field are massively out of work. The stagnant real estate market will affect to the other relative production fields such as construction materials, interior goods, ... The unemployment rate in the society increases, the people limit the expenditure. The price of goods in the markets has the sign of reducing strongly and of course, the profit level of the enterprises reduces continuously. The average rate of return of the enterprises also reduces thereof, and if the commodity price reduces continuously, the average rate of return of the enterprises can reduce lower than the input interest rate of the bank. *This stage is shown by section 3-4 in figure 1.6.*

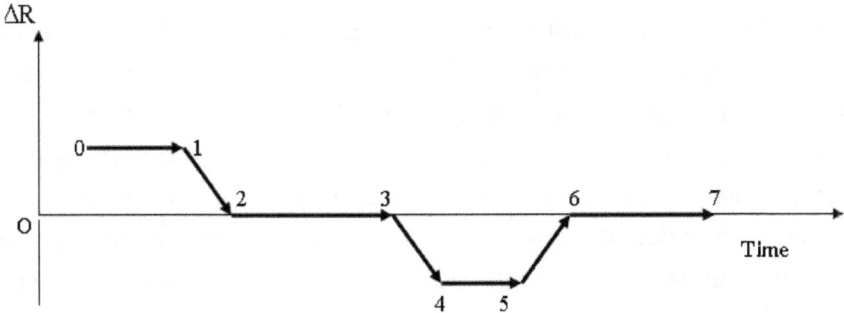

Figure 1.6 (2nd re-draw for follow advantageously): The relative change of average rate of return of business block comparing with banking interest rate (ΔR) through different development stages of economic cycle

The low investment effect makes the production scale of the economy narrow gradually. After a period of adjusting, the commodity price and production scale establish the bottom level and not reducing. The economy gets the new temporary equilibrium state, called **cold equilibrium state**, at that time, the average rate of return of the enterprises can be lower than the level of saving deposit interest rate. Normally, when the commodity price level reduces, the bank interest rate will reduce, but when the economy is taken ill, the belief reduces, the overdue debt increases in the banks, so reducing the interest rate will be hard to attract the idle balances in the people. The interest rate only reduces if having the intervention by the Government through the policy of the loose currency. However, here we temporarily don't count the role of the Government, we want consider the method of self-adjusting of the economy. The economy continues to operate normally at new temporary equilibrium state, in which the price stabilizes at low level and saving interest rate is rather attractive. *This stage is shown by section 4-5 in figure 1.6.*

In next period, the enterprises re-arrange the business operation; the banks recover the belief of the customers. Households and economic organizations which have the idle balances, are afraid of risks before, but now they bring money to deposit in the bank to enjoy the interest. The area of business operation doesn't have new changes; lending debit balance can't increase, the input interest rate trends to reduce gradually, bringing about the similar reduction at lending interest rate. Such interest rate development is very convenient for business operation. On the other hand, when the interest rate reduces and the belief in the economy increases, people are fiery with consumption and this pushes up the price of commodity. The price of commodity increases, this improves the profit of the enterprises. The enterprises continue to mobilize the capital, expand the business scale to increase the profit. The unemployment in the society reduces, the commodity yield increases and can get the equal level with the period of before happening the economic shock. *This stage is shown by section 5-6 in figure 1.6.*

Commodity price increases at suitable level, after that enters into stability and equilibrium with commodity yield. Bank interest rate can increase little and establish new platform. The average rate of return of the enterprises is in the middle of the input and output interest rate of the banks. At this time, the economy returns to **stable equilibrium state**. *This stage is shown by section 6-7 in figure 1.6.*

Summarize above analyses we find that, the economy trends to change continuously in long-term, but it can equilibrate temporarily in short-term. At short-term equilibrium states, the price of commodity, interest rate and yield level is relative stable. Figure 1.6 shows the process of relative change of the average rate of return of the enterprises according to the time correlative with changes of the economy through some short-term equilibrium states analyzed above.

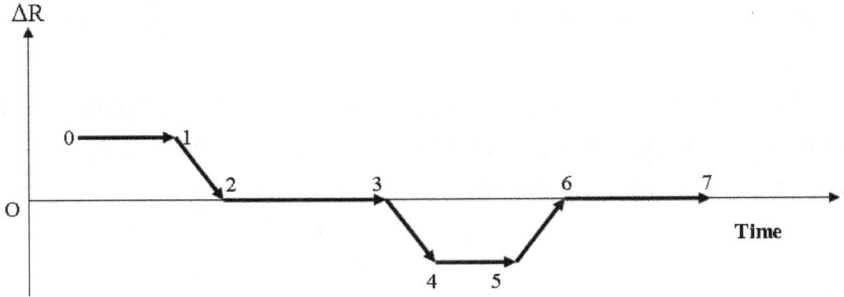

Figure 1.6 (3rd re-draw for follow advantageously): The relative change of average rate of return of business block comparing with banking interest rate (ΔR) through different development stages of economic cycle

(0-1) is the temporary equilibrium state, in which the price, yield, interest rate and average rate of return of the enterprises are at high level, we call this *hot equilibrium state*. (1-2) is the adjusting stage of the economy. (2-3) is *stable equilibrium state*, there the yield, price, interest rate reduce comparing with hot equilibrium state. At this equilibrium state, the average rate of return of the enterprises is equal to arithmetic average of the input and output interest rate of the bank. (3-4) shows the depression stage of the economy. (4-5) is *cold equilibrium state*, the yield, price and interest rate here are low. (5-6) is the stage of rehabilitating the economy. (6-7) is new *stable equilibrium state*, the yield, price and interest rate here rehabilitate strongly comparing with the bottom (4-5).

Finally, we return the main content of this section that is to try to answer the question: where is the average profit of the enterprises? As we know, at hot equilibrium state of the economy, the average rate of return of the enterprises is higher than the output interest rate of the bank. At the cold equilibrium state, the average rate of return of the enterprises is lower than the input interest rate at the bank. And at the stable equilibrium states, the average rate of return of the enterprises is between the input and output interest rate of the bank. So, if consider in the long-term, the average rate of return of the enterprises is equal to arithmetic average of input interest rate and output interest rate of the bank.

If call R_1 long-term average input interest rate of the bank, call R_2 long-term average lending interest rate of the bank, call R_{DN} long-term average rate of return of the enterprises, we have:

$$R_{DN} = \frac{R_1 + R_2}{2}$$

In a close and perfect competitive market economy, long-term average rate of return of all enterprises is equal to arithmetic average of long-term average interest rate at input and output of system of commercial banks.

For example: in a long-term period, if $R_1 = 8\%$, $R_2 = 12\%$ then $R_{DN} = 10\%$. Or $R_1 = 3\%$, $R_2 = 6\%$, then $R_{DN} = 4.5\%$.

We try calculating R_{DN} in 5 years with the data as following:

	1st year	2nd year	3rd year	4th year	5th year
Average mobilizing interest rate of bank system	5%	4%	6%	7%	3%
Average lending interest rate of bank system	8%	7%	9%	10%	6%

We have: $R_1 = \dfrac{5\% + 4\% + 6\% + 7\% + 3\%}{5} = 5\%$

$R_2 = \dfrac{8\% + 7\% + 9\% + 10\% + 6\%}{5} = 8\%$

$R_{DN} = \dfrac{R_1 + R_2}{2} = \dfrac{5\% + 8\%}{2} = 6.5\%$

At the beginning of this section, we suppose about the model of the market economy which is close, perfect competitive and bears little influence by the Government. In fact, the regulation of the Government in the market economy changes only the adjusting time of each hot or cold stage of the economic cycle, it can't level the cycles or keep the economy at fixed equilibrium state. Therefore, macroeconomic regulating role of the Government doesn't affect much long-term average rate of return of business block. In an economy which doesn't have perfect competition in some fields, the average rate of return in those fields is bigger than that in other fields and this can affect the common average rate of return of all the enterprises. In an open economy, investors can select the suitable place in different countries to execute the business project with the highest effect. Besides that, open trade relation makes wrong our analyses on economic cycle mentioned above. Therefore, in an open economy, the average rate of return of the enterprises depends on the competitive ability of domestic business block in the world market.

1.8 Price and commodity value

We start by brief and clear concepts.

1. In common meaning, **commodity** is any product transacted, bought and sold in the market. Commodity is divided in at least 4 kinds: physical commodity, service commodity, super-commodity and secondary commodity.

2. **Physical commodity** is a physical product with particular use and traded in the market, they have the origin from the nature constituted by labor of human. For example: rice, coal, domestic water, television, antibiotic,...

3. **Service commodity** is a spirit product or right of using temporarily a particular product, right of being guided, cared from someone, all trade in the market. For example, watch the music program, travel, rent the house, rent the car, tutor, ...

4. **Super-commodity** is the complexes of commodity – service which is big, multifunction, traded in the market. For example, enterprises, hospitals, ports, ...

5. **Secondary commodity** is instruments of finance, vouchers of confirming assets ownership by money, ordinary commodity or a part of ordinary commodity, traded in the market. For example, enterprise share, public bond, futures contract, ...

6. In the market economy, **commodity value** shows at economic value, calculating by money amount and decided by manufacturers – distributors.

7. **Commodity price** is the exchange value through transaction, calculating by money amount and decided by the market.

The topic on price and commodity value is paid attention because it brings the practicability in the life and has special economic meaning. Perhaps you leant about different concepts related to this content, but here we analyze according to another method and infer the important results.

As mentioned above the commodity is divided into many different kinds, each kind has specific characteristics, so determining the value of commodity can't observe a common formula. In this section, we mention only determining the value of general kinds of physical commodity and service commodity.

1.8.1 Proper value of commodity

In the market economy, there are many different fields of business operation to meet the diversified demand of people. Each field of business operation has many competitive enterprises to affirm the post in the business world. Each enterprise has specific production technology, certain management ability and particular sales method. The commodity of an enterprise has the common features and different features with enterprises in same field. We start this topic by determining the proper value of commodity.

In previous sections, we determined the expense of business operation of the enterprise (P_{sx-kd}) by accumulating three kinds of expense: manpower expense, material resources expense and derived expense. That is total expense to produce and distribute the commodity quantity Q of the enterprise. So we are easy to calculate the expense of business operation for a commodity unit by dividing total expense by commodity yield Q.

If call p^k_{sx-kd} expense of business operation for a commodity unit of a typical enterprise K, we have:

$$p^k_{sx-kd} = \frac{P^k_{sx-kd}}{Q_k}$$

In which: P^k_{sx-kd} is total expense of business operation of enterprise K in a certain period, Q_k is commodity quantity produced and sold in that period.

In reality, there are many enterprises which produce and trade in same commodity type, each enterprise applies particular production technology and secret, different method of marketing and sales, so the expense of business operation for a commodity unit will be different.

In before section, we know that the long-term average rate of return of the enterprises (R_{DN}) in entire economy is equal to arithmetic average of the input and output interest rate of the bank. However, because of severe competition among the enterprises in same production field and among fields, the rate of return of each field of production and each enterprise is different; it can be bigger, equal or smaller than R_{DN}.

Call V_k necessary commodity price so that enterprise K which we are considering, gets the rate of return equal to the average rate of return of the enterprises R_{DN}. Here V_k is only supposed price, it is not necessary equal to real price of commodity in the market. We have following formula:

Supposed profit of the enterprise $M_k = V_k \times Q_k - p^k_{sx-kd} \times Q_k = (V_k - p^k_{sx-kd})Q_k$

Supposed the rate of return of the enterprise $R_k = \dfrac{M_k}{I_k} \times 100\% =$

$$\frac{(V_k - p^k_{sx-kd})Q_k}{I_k} \times 100\% = R_{DN}$$

In which, I_k is equity of the enterprise, Q_k is commodity yield consumed in a year, p^k_{sx-kd} is expense of business operation for a commodity unit.

From above formula, we have: $(V_k - p^k_{sx-kd})Q_k = I_k \times R_{DN}$ → $V_k - p^k_{sx-kd} = \dfrac{I_k R_{DN}}{Q_k}$

→ $V_k = p^k_{sx-kd} + \dfrac{I_k R_{DN}}{Q_k}$

Value V_k reflects the expense of business operation with specific characteristic in each enterprise and contains a profit level enough for the enterprise to get the rate of return equal to the average rate of return R_{DN}. V_k is called **proper value of commodity** produced by enterprise K. In reality, if product sale price of enterprise K is bigger than proper value of commodity V_k the rate of return of the enterprise is bigger than average rate of return R_{DN}. If product sale price is equal or lower than V_k the rate of return of enterprise K is equal or lower than R_{DN}.

Commodity value in circulation

In the market economy, there is division of labor at high level. Manufacturers concentrate in raising the productivity, quality of products and marketing, spreading in the market. Normally, they find only big distribution clues to deliver without executing all process of distributing commodity. Professional distribution system executes the duty of transporting commodity from production enterprise to the final users everywhere. Commodity distribution system can include many intermediate stages, so retail price of commodity can be higher much than factory cost of the manufacturer.

Commodity distributors are specific enterprises with similar input and output factors, if they are different, the difference is only time and delivery place. Commodity distribution clues don't change the shape, structure or quality of products, but they must provide capital for business, transport expense, yard expense to collect commodity, expense of market research and manpower for sales. So, commodity although produced only in a fixed place, is presented and appeared around the world.

Commodity distributors are also business units, distribution activity is free, so the idle capital resource in the society can be put in production or investment of expanding the distribution system. In the stable conditions of the market, the average rate of return of distribution field is correlative to other fields of business operation.

We consider a distribution enterprise A, this distributor imports many different kinds of commodity and resell in the market. Suppose that, in the commodities imported by distributor A there is commodity B produced by enterprise K. Import price of commodity B is P_k. To distribute a commodity B, enterprise A must bear the expense p_k^a. Call m_k^a necessary profit of enterprise A collected on a commodity unit B so that the rate of return of enterprise A is equal to R_{DN}. Call V_k^a proper value of commodity B at output of enterprise A. We have:

$$V_k^a = P_k + p_k^a + m_k^a$$

Suppose in long-term, average commodity B price of enterprise K for distributor A is equal proper value V_k determined by enterprise K, it means $P_k = V_k$.

So: $V_k^a = V_k + p_k^a + m_k^a$.

From above formula, we find that through the intermediate distribution stage, the proper value of commodity rises. The more intermediate stages there are, the higher the proper value of commodity is pushed. In reality, distribution field also has severe competition to exist and control the market share, so intermediate stages of the distribution system will reduce according to the time and finally form an irreducible distribution system.

1.8.2 Average value of a variety of commodity

In the competitive market, many manufacturers bring together out market a kind of commodity which is similar about size, shape, use, etc, we call it a variety of commodity. A commodity item is divided into many groups of commodity; each group of commodity includes many varieties of commodity. For example, rice has 2 groups: ordinary rice and sticky rice, each group of ordinary rice or sticky rice has not less 10 different varieties of rice. Television item includes many groups of commodity such as television using image tube, LCD television, Plasma television,... Each group of television also includes many varieties such as television 14", 21", 25",... New drug item can include hundreds groups of commodity, vitamin is a group of commodity, acid ascorbic is a variety of commodity under group of vitamin, there are tens of different acid ascorbic supplied by many manufacturers.

We consider a variety of commodity B. There are N enterprises in same field producing variety of commodity B, each enterprise has specific technology, so production expense is different.

Call V_k proper value of commodity produced by k-th enterprise (k = 1....N). Call Q_k commodity quantity consumed by k-th enterprise in a year. Call V_o average value of variety of commodity B. We have:

$$V_o = \frac{\sum V_k Q_k}{\sum Q_k}$$

Suppose that N enterprises sell commodity B in the market with different price subject to particular property on the product produced by each enterprise, but average price is equal to V_o. We try calculating the rate of return of entire field including N enterprises to consider the result.

$$R = \frac{\sum M_k}{\sum I_k}$$, In which R is the rate of return of entire field; M_k, I_k is

in turn profit and investment capital of k-th enterprise.

$M_k = P_k \times Q_k - p^k_{sx-kd} \times Q_k = (P_k - p^k_{sx-kd}) Q_k$ in which, P_k is product sale price of k-th enterprise, p^k_{sx-kd} is expense of business operation for a commodity product of k-th enterprise.

→ $\sum M_k = \sum (P_k - p^k_{sx-kd})Q_k = \sum P_k Q_k - \sum p^k_{sx-kd} Q_k$

Because of supposing V_o as average sale price of N enterprises so $\sum P_k Q_k = V_o \times \sum Q_k$

V_o is also average value of variety of commodity B, so: $V_o \times \sum Q_k = \sum V_k Q_k$

→ $\sum M_k = \sum P_k Q_k - \sum p^k_{sx-kd} Q_k = \sum V_k Q_k - \sum p^k_{sx-kd} Q_k = \sum (V_k - p^k_{sz-kd})Q_k$

We find that $(V_k - p^k_{sx-kd})Q_k$ is the profit of k-th enterprise when $P_k = V_k$ that is also the profit enough to k-th enterprise having rate of return equal to R_{DN}.

If put $(V_k - p^k_{sx-kd})Q_k = M_k^o$ we have:

$$R = \frac{\sum M_k}{\sum I_k} = \frac{\sum M_k^0}{\sum I_k}, \text{ because } \frac{M_k^0}{I_k} \text{ is equal with every k}$$

from 1....N and equal to R_{DN} so:

$$R = \frac{\sum M_k^0}{\sum I_k} = R_{DN}$$

Finally we find that, if average sale price of enterprises is equal to average commodity value V_o, the rate of return of entire field is equal to R_{DN}.

1.8.3 Average price of a variety of commodity

We continue the variety of commodity B mentioned above.

Call P_o average price of the variety of commodity B, call P_k and Q_k is in turn product sale price and sold commodity volume of k-th enterprise, with k = 1...N. We have:

$$P_o = \frac{\sum P_k Q_k}{\sum Q_k}$$

If $P_o = V_o$, it means average commodity price is equal to average commodity value, the rate of return of entire field of producing variety of commodity B is equal to R_{DN}. Then investment effect in field of producing commodity B is equal to average level of the economy.

Among N enterprises producing commodity B, the enterprise which has high rate of return will continue to expand investment to increase the profit and market share, the enterprises which have low rate of return will narrow the production to raise the effect. Perhaps some weak enterprises will leave out this field to change to other field of production, and some enterprises in other fields change to invest, produce commodity B. In general, in this case, production field of commodity B is in equilibrium state, investment capital flow and commodity yield supplying to the market are always stable, supply and demand is equilibrium and the price changes little. We call it is equilibrium state of a production field.

Put: $P_o = c_o V_o$ in which, c_o is coefficient of reflecting the supply and demand in the market of commodity B.

When $c_o = 1$ we have $P_o = V_o$, then the commodity market is equilibrium, we have supply is equal to demand.

When $c_o > 1$ we have $P_o > V_o$, it means average commodity price of entire field is bigger than average commodity value of entire field, the rate of return of entire field is bigger than average rate of return of the economy. At that time, with market of commodity B, supply is smaller than demand.

When $c_o < 1$ we have $P_o < V_o$, it means average commodity price of entire field is smaller than average commodity value of entire field, the rate of return of entire field is smaller than average rate of return of the economy. At that time, with market of commodity B, supply is bigger than demand.

1.8.4 Proper price of commodity

Each enterprise has different production technology, the commodity in the same variety has particular features, although in general they are similar. For example, consider a kind of commodity, namely television LCD 32". There are many firms producing together this variety of commodity such as: Samsung, LG, Sony, Panasonic, Sanyo, Toshiba,.... Look at the appearance, the products of firms are similar, but consider carefully there are differences about sharp level, control software, warranty, ... And of course, the price is different. The specific unique features on the product can create the special consumption effect, make the price increase higher than commodity of the same variety. Although produce the product in same variety, each firm tries to create the particular impression for customers. That is about product quality, marketing method or way of taking care of the customers.

Call P_k price of commodity B produced by enterprise k in the field.

Put $P_k = c_k P_o$ in which: P_o is average price of commodity B in the entire field, c_k is the coefficient of reflecting particular supply and demand of k-th enterprise in the market of commodity B.

If $c_k = 1$ then $P_k = P_o$, price of commodity B produced by enterprise k is equal to average price of entire field.

If $c_k > 1$ then $P_k > P_o$, price of commodity B produced by enterprise k is bigger than average price of entire field.

If $c_k < 1$ then $P_k < P_o$, price of commodity B produced by enterprise k is smaller than average price of entire field.

From $P_k = c_k P_o$ and $P_o = c_o V_o$ → $P_k = c_k c_o V_o$ in which: V_o is average value of variety of commodity B, c_o is coefficient of reflecting the supply and demand in the market of commodity B.

From previous parts, we have: $V_k = p^k_{sx\text{-}kd} + \dfrac{I_k R_{DN}}{Q_k}$

When $P_k = V_k$, it means price of commodity is equal to its value, the enterprise gets the rate of return equal to R_{DN}.

From $V_k = p^k_{sx\text{-}kd} + \dfrac{I_k R_{DN}}{Q_k}$ → $V_k - p^k_{sx\text{-}kd} = \dfrac{I_k R_{DN}}{Q_k}$

Put $m_o = V_k - p^k_{sx\text{-}kd} = \dfrac{I_k R_{DN}}{Q_k}$, m_o is the profit on a commodity unit when the enterprise has the rate of return equal to R_{DN}.

Put $m = P_k - p^k_{sx\text{-}kd}$, this is real profit on a commodity unit.

Put $\Delta m = m - m_o = (P_k - p^k_{sx\text{-}kd}) - (V_k - p^k_{sx\text{-}kd}) = P_k - V_k = c_k c_o V_o - V_k =$

$$c_k c_o V_o - p^k_{sx-kd} - \frac{I_k R_{DN}}{Q_k}$$

Δm is called **competitive profit** on a commodity unit (competitive profit of enterprise for short). If Δm > 0 it proves the enterprise has good competitive capacity and at that time the enterprise gets **superprofit**. Value Δm < 0 warns about bad competitive capacity of the enterprise comparing with other competitors in the market. Δm = 0 shows that the enterprise has average competitive capacity in entire field.

From formula $\Delta m = c_k c_o V_o - p^k_{sx-kd} - \frac{I_k R_{DN}}{Q_k}$, we find that $I_k R_{DN}$ is known before and invariable, c_o and V_o are specific values for entire production field and if there is change, it will affect whole the field. Therefore, each enterprise wants to increase the profit in general and value Δm in particular, the enterprise must increase consumption yield Q_k, decrease production expense p^k_{sx-kd} and increase proper coefficient of supply and demand c_k.

1.9 Supply, demand and price change

According to common principle, when we mention the supply and demand of a kind of commodity, it means we want to mention the real supply ability of the enterprise and effective demand of buyer, to eliminate the phenomenon of imaginary supply or imaginary demand. Supply and demand are not specific figures but are functions of describing the behavior tendency of seller and buyer in the market. However, volume of supply and volume of demand are the clear figures.

Volume of supply is the commodity quantity which supplier wants to sell at a specific price and in a determined period.

Volume of demand is the commodity quantity which buyer wants to buy at a specific price and in a determined period.

With a price level and period set before, manufacturers will bring out the market a specific commodity volume of supply suitable for the capacity and production effect. Similarly, with a price level and fixed period, buyer will consider and select the suitable commodity quantity to buy.

The period of surveying the volume of supply or volume of demand is subject to the desire of researcher and property of commodity. With items such as food, foodstuff, the surveying period can be daily or according to long or short time. With most of ordinary items, we can survey according to week, month, quarter or year. With the market of automobile or real estate, the surveying period at least is a month, even years, the collected data really has meaning.

Supply is general function to denote a set of volume of supply when the commodity price changes and surveying period is constant.

Demand is general function to denote a set of volume of demand when the commodity price changes and surveying period is constant.

Constant period plays the important role for surveying volume of supply and volume of demand when the price changes. When the period changes, the changes about investment capital flow, production technology will affect the supply and the changes about taste and income affect the demand.

1.9.1 Supply line and demand line

The simplest method to understand about supply and demand is to show them by graphs. We don't hope to have the exact graphs because we don't have enough specific figures but only expected figures on volume of supply or volume of demand. The supply line or demand line will be the imitating lines with sketch. However, they still show the nature of seller and buyer in the market.

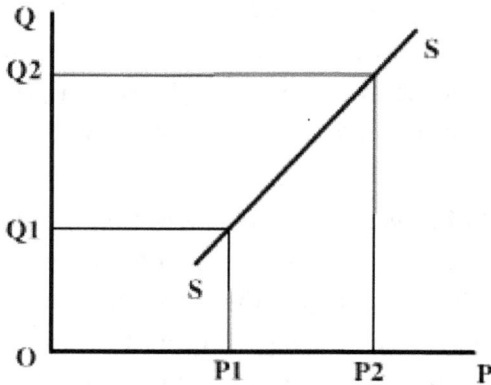

Figure 1.7: Supply line SS

With the low price, few enterprises want to supply the product, so the volume of supply is small; at low price level P1 we have small volume of supply Q1. When the price increases, the volume of supply also increases, at price level P2 > P1 we have the correlative volume of supply Q2 > Q1. The supply line SS in figure 1.7 shows the changes of volume of supply when the price changes.

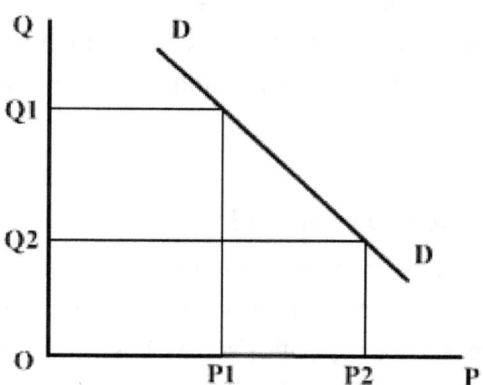

Figure 1.8: Demand line DD

Contrary to the supply, the cheaper commodity price is, the more buyers are and the bigger the volume of supply is, at low price level P1 we have rather high volume of supply Q1. When the price level increases, buyers decrease and volume of supply decreases, at price level P2 > P1 we have volume of demand Q2 < Q1. Demand line DD in figure 1.8 describes the change of commodity volume of demand when the price level changes.

1.9.2 Short-term equilibrium state

Now we remember the variety of commodity B mentioned in previous parts and continue analyzing the relation of supply and demand in the market by the graphs. Firstly, imitate the supply line and demand line on commodity B in next 1 month. We had the data related to the situation of supply and demand of commodity B in last 1 month. The average price level and consumption yield of variety of commodity B in last 1 month is in turn P_o and Q_o. Suppose that, at present, we find that no reason can change the market of commodity B comparing with last month. So, the supply line and demand line on commodity B imitating for next month preserve comparing with last month. Two lines of supply and demand (SS and DD) of commodity B show together on a coordinate system intersecting at point $G(P_o, Q_o)$ as in figure 1.9.

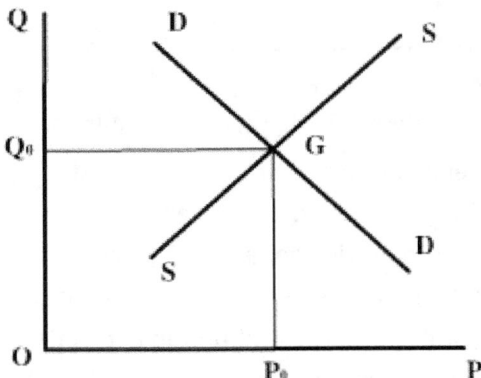

Figure 1.9: Short-term equilibrium market

At point G volume of supply is equal to volume of demand, besides no point satisfies such condition. With price levels more than P_o volume of supply is bigger than volume of demand and at price levels less than P_o volume of demand is bigger than volume of supply. P_o is short-term equilibrium price of market of commodity B.

1.9.3 The shift of supply line

Suppose that variety of commodity B is a kind of ordinary rice. In last several months, the rice market in the world and in Vietnam is relative stable, The supply line and the demand line on rice in Vietnamese market with period of 1 month is always stable. Monthly average price is P_o(VND/kg) and consumption yield in the month is Q_o(kg). At this moment, we also survey the supply line and demand line on rice within next 30 days and find that they don't change comparing with last month.

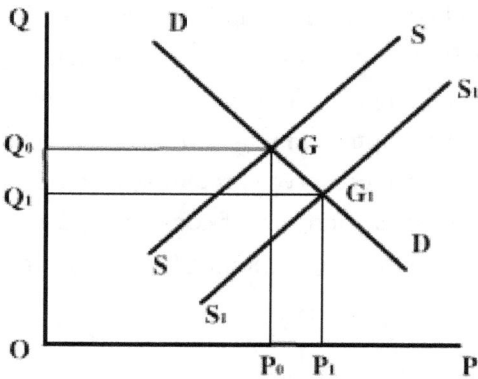

Figure 1.10: Supply line shift

But after a week, a strong storm happens suddenly in the southern of South China Sea. This storm affects provinces in Southern Vietnam and Thailand, many main rice zones have a bad harvest. The news on the storm is spread and it affects the rice market at once. Rice suppliers understand what will happen in next period and start to limit sell rice to the market. From this moment, short-term supply line (1 month) on the rice changes. At each price level, volume of supply will decrease and supply line SS shifts to the right of the graph to position S_1S_1 as in figure 1.10. In general, demand line on rice in next month is stable; it means the line DD is constant. Two lines of supply and demand in next month intersect at point G_1 correlative to new price level P_1 and consumption yield Q_1. At new equilibrium point of rice market, the price increases and consumption commodity quantity reduces.

Market Economy & Policy On Two Domestic Currencies

Suppose that the storm doesn't appear, but there is the information on a main crop more abundant than usual in Southeast Asia, the short-term supply line SS, in stead of shifting to the right, will shift to the left of the graph and establish new equilibrium point with demand line at point G_2 correlative to price level $P_2 < P_o$ and yield $Q_2 > Q_o$.

Besides the reasons on weather affecting main crops shifts the supply line, there are many other reasons affecting similarly. For example, applying new rice variety increases the productivity leading to increasing supply resource or using the progressive cultivating technology reduces the input expense and increases the supply resource. But the industrialization wave overflows into rural area, this will lead to narrow the agricultural land and reduce the ability of supplying rice.

1.9.4 The shift of demand line

We continue on the rice market. In previous months, suppose that the rice market is equilibrium at point $G(P_o, Q_o)$, and at present the market is stable and two lines of supply and demand for next month is preserved.

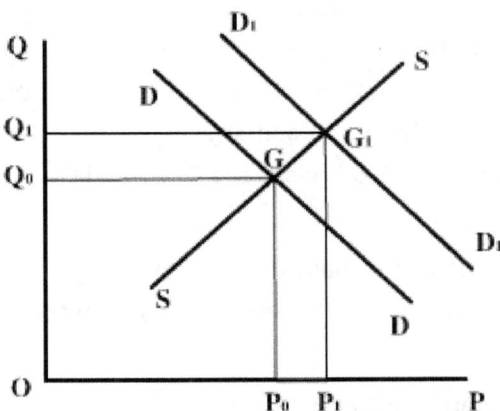

Figure 1.11: Demand line shift

We suppose that new event happening in the week is the fact Organization of Petroleum Exporting Countries OPEC suddenly cuts strongly the exploiting yield, make the price of crude oil increase. When the crude oil price increases, some developed countries use cereals as raw material for refining the biological oil to replace the ordinary oil. The oil price is high; more maize is put into factories of preparing biological petrol. The maize price in the market increases gradually and it becomes expensive comparing with other kinds of cereals, many people intend to use other kinds of cereals in stead of maize such as rice or wheat, make demand on rice increase. Therefore, now with each price level set before, the correlative volume of demand on rice will increase. The demand line DD in next month will shift to the right to the position D_1D_1 as in figure 1.11. The unusual price increase of maize affect only demand on rice, not affect the rice supply resource, so the supply line SS for next month is preserved. Two lines of supply and demand for next month intersect at point G1 correlative to price level $P_1>P_o$ and $Q_1>Q_o$. At new equilibrium point of rice market, both of price level and consumption yield increase.

Another script can happen to the rice market. Suppose that in previous months the rice market is still equilibrium at point G (P_o,Q_o) and the next month is expected to not change. However, a problem happens suddenly. Scientists discover the pesticide in rice exceeding the permitted level. Therefore, the careful customers change from using rice to using wheat, the demand on rice reduces. Demand line DD will shift to the left of the graph and supply line SS preserves. These lines will intersect at point G_2 correlative to $P_2<P_o$ and $Q_2<Q_o$.

In reality, there are many reasons affecting the rice demand and shifting the demand line to the left or the right of the graph.

1.9.5 Long-term equilibrium state

We have just surveyed the rice market in short-term, in particular in a month. With such short period, when happen a shock on the supply, the supply line shifts strongly, the demand line preserves, or a shock on the demand, the demand line shifts strongly, the supply line preserves. However, in stead of surveying in a month, we survey the rice market in a next year; the situation will have many changes. The problem is, in short-term the market doesn't have enough time to react with big shock happening suddenly, in long-term both supply and demand change to adapt to the market development. Return to the example on the rice market and the shift of supply line to the right when the storm causes bad crops. Therefore, in short-term the supply resource is scarce and rice price increases. After the rice price increases, farmers in areas which doesn't happen the natural calamity find that the rice price is rather expensive and profitable for the crops, they try to take care of rice better than before to hope to get high productivity, both of having a good crop and having high price. Other farmers, who left rice to grow vegetables and crops before, now find the change they return to work before. Therefore, both of productivity and area of rice for next crop can increase strongly enough compensate for deficiency on rice damaged by severe storm in last crop of rice. So, in medium-term, volume of supply on rice will increase and can restore the yield as high as the yield before the storm happens. Supply line SS after shifting to the right because of the shock on supply, now shifts to the left, back to position before.

Clearly, short-term equilibrium state and long-term equilibrium state is different, we need to take account of them when survey the commodity markets. In short-term, the contingent factors often affect the development of supply and demand but in long-term the real demand of buyer and business effect of seller will decide the supply and demand in the market.

Now, we survey together the rice market in long-term, particularly in a year. Suppose that the lines of supply and demand in last year is SS and DD as in the figure 1.12, concurrently G_0 is long-term equilibrium point of the market in last year, correlative to average price P_0 and rice yield consumed in the year is Q_0.

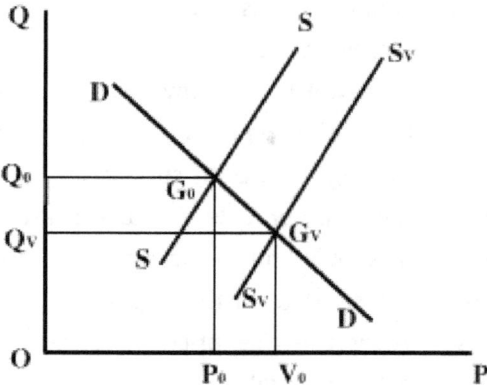

Figure 1.12: Long-term equilibrium market

Call V_o average value of rice kind in next year. Suppose that in next time, price of input items for rice production doesn't change such as price of fertilizer, rice variety, wages, ... Need to suppose additionally the stable natural conditions as previous years. Like this, in next year, average value of rice preserves and equal to average value of rice in previous year. Compare two values P_o and V_o to infer the important results. If P_o is lower than V_o, it means average price of rice in last year is lower than average value of rice. Then average rate of return of rice production field is lower than average rate of return of entire economy. Because rice manufacturers such as farmers, cooperatives, farms, plantations apply the different production technology, different input expense, therefore the rate of return is different. In reality, there is a section of rice manufacturers incurring losses or have low business effect. Therefore, the area of growing rice runs the risk of reducing in next rice crops because some farmers who grew rice but no effect, change to grow other agricultural products. Supply resource of rice in long-term will reduce and supply line SS shifts to the right of the graph. Consider the demand on rice in long-term, suppose that there is no unusual thing and demand line on rice preserves. When the line SS shifts to the right, the rice price increases gradually and consumption yield reduces.

Notice that when a group of farmers who work with bad effect must change from growing rice to growing other farm produce, the rice yield reduces and average value of rice reduces. Two values P_o and V_o change in reverse order, when P_o increases, V_o reduces. Supply line SS doesn't shift unlimited to the right, it will stop when $P_o = V_o$.

We continue to survey the rice market within 1 year, but this time, there are changes from demand. We continue to suppose that the rice market in last year is equilibrium at point G_0 with the supply line SS and demand line DD as in figure 1.13. Average price of rice in last year is P_0 lower than average value V_0. Suppose that conditions related to rice production is constant, the average value of rice in next year is equal to V_0. As above, we find the supply line SS will shift to the right so that average price moves towards equal to its value.

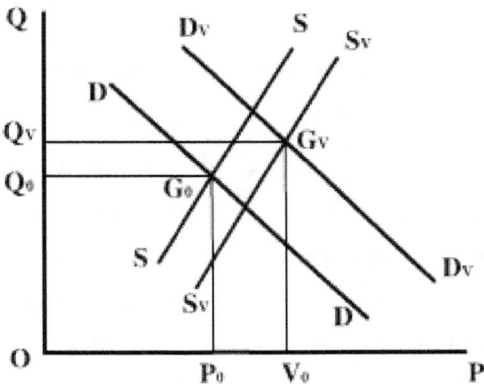

Figure 1.13 Long-term equilibrium market

Now we continue to consider the rice demand. Because the price of petrol escalates, a big quantity of cereals is used into the goal of preparing the biological petrol, so the price of maize, soybeans increases. Many people change from using other kinds of cereals with high price to using rice, so the demand on rice increases. If this situation is not temporary but long-term, the demand line on rice in next year will shift much to the right of the graph. Suppose the line DD to shift to the new position D_vD_v as in figure. The line SS will shift gradually to the right according to the time until average price is equal to value V_0 and then it stops. Suppose that the line SS shifts to new position S_vS_v. Two lines of supply and demand for next year as S_vS_v and D_vD_v intersect at point G_v correlative to new price $P = V_0$, and yield $Q = Q_v$. Notice that, because the supply yield in next year changes from Q_0 to Q_v, average value of rice in next year has the change with average value of rice in previous year.

In brief, in short-term the market changes strongly because of the shocks, in long-term, the market changes with more basic characteristics. The income ability and the taste of customers will be the motive power to shift the demand line, average value of commodity is the centre attracting the shift direction of supply line. In long-term, the market is equilibrium at the position which average price of the commodity is equal to its average value.

1.10 Operation law of market economy

In daily life, economic activities hold the most of time fund of each of us. Select goods when shop, work in an enterprise, calculate the daily expenditure or research the investment plans, all they are related to money, rice – economic values. The market economy is severe competition, all parts in the market economy must observe its operation laws to exist and develop. The operation law of the market economy uses the value of currency as the motive power and the market is the arbitrator to fix the final result of the competition. Competition for the economic target is the basic factor which helps the market economy regulate by itself and get the equilibrium state in short-term as well as long-term.

1.10.1 Benefit equilibrium in each individual

Each individual has the particular ability on health, intelligence, personality, aptitude and assets. The market economy has high freedom, the scopes of business are diversified with many types of enterprises. Individuals, subject to the ability, select their job as employee or employer. The enterprises must compete severely to exist, they appreciate the manpower. Through the labor market, each person can select a favorite job with suitable salary; the enterprises recruit the personnel team with suitable ability and competitive salary.

1.10.2 Benefit equilibrium in family

Each family has own budget, it is formed from the income of members in the family. Those items can include salary, bonus, interest + saving principal and interest + investment capital. Families must plan to allocate the budget for usual expenditure, buying durable goods and a part for savings or contributing capital for business. With limited budget, families are careful in selecting the necessary consumption goods – services to get the optimal satisfaction. The price of commodity in the market is formed naturally through the rub between buyer and seller. The equilibrium price of commodity shows their social value. There are some factors affecting plan of allocating the budget of families. First is the inflation which reduces the purchasing power of currency and each family must spend more money to receive the commodity volume as before. The rate of allocating expenditure also changes because price level changes unequally among items. If saving interest increases, households will consider more carefully between buying durable commodity for using today and depositing for saving to buy more in another moment.

1.10.3 Benefit equilibrium in each enterprise

Each enterprise must plan an effective business strategy to compete with competitors in the same scope. They need to promote the own strength to impress on the product from quality, price to serving style. To collect high profit, enterprises must reduce production expense suitably, raise the commodity quality and strengthen advertisement marketing to improve the specific coefficient of supply and demand in the market. In the process, subject to the profit, each enterprise has the reasonable behavior to optimize the profit or limit the loss. The enterprises which have the rate of return lower than interest rate of saving deposit must raise the competitive ability, if not they must narrow the production and dismiss employees. The enterprises which have the rate of return in the middle of average interest rate of input and output of the banks are ranked in average grade. These enterprises, although don't want to expand the scale of enterprise, not to go as far as to narrow the production or cut the manpower. Group of leading enterprises of entire field has the rate of return higher than average output interest rate of the bank. They want to expand the business scale to increase the profit by own fund or borrowing. When the enterprise still has the ability to increase the profit, the enterprise has the motive power to increase the supply yield. The enterprise stops temporarily swelling out when the marginal profit is equal to expense of borrowing capital, in other words, when marginal revenue is equal to total marginal expense, the enterprise stops temporarily expanding the production scale.

1.10.4 Benefit equilibrium in business operation sector

In the same field of production, enterprises compete to affirm the position and trademark. Different fields of production have no direct reason to confront in the market, social capital flow allocated into each field is not fix but adapt oneself to the circumstances. The economy has many different scopes, because the changes on supply and demand happen continuously, the situation of business operation in each field has certain advantages and difficulties. The rate of return among fields distributes unequally according to the time, therefore, the investment capital flow is always asked with insistence from this field to other field. The fields of business operation which the average rate of return of entire field is bigger than R_{DN} and have growing prospect will be taken special interest by the society. The quick-witted investors find the way of narrowing production at fields which are not effective in order to concentrate the resources into places having good profit. The social capital flow shifts to the direction of increasing the profit and reducing the risk for itself. The scale of promising fields will be expanded until the rate of return of entire field reduces and equal to average rate of return R_{DN}. The bad fields of business operation will narrow the scale, reduce the yield until the rate of return of the field increases gradually and get the value equal to R_{DN}.

1.10.5 Macro-equilibrium

We divide the economy into two sectors: sector of production and sector of consumption. The macro-equilibrium shows at the equilibrium of total supply and total demand in gross domestic product (GDP). In normal economic conditions, the situation of market price is stable, the equilibrium yield of supply and demand and people's income are stable. When happen the change on supply or demand, because of any reason, also affect macro-equilibrium of the economy. Hereafter we will survey the model of total supply and total demand of the economy in different periods: short-term, medium-term and long-term; when the economic background changes. Time for short-term or long-term is subject to the real condition and determined by surveyor. With the proper supposition on time convention for this section as following: short-term is 6 months, medium-term is 12 months and long-term is 24 months.

Short-term equilibrium

Suppose that the economy is at short-term equilibrium state expected with line of total supply SS and line of total demand DD intersecting at G_0, correlative to yield Q_0 and average price P_0 as in figure 1.14. The important matter is, when appear the shocks changing from supply or demand, how does the economy behave to re-establish the new equilibrium state? We consider the event of a country just joining in WTO for example. Besides the event of joining in WTO, suppose that in survey time, other conditions of the economy have few changes.

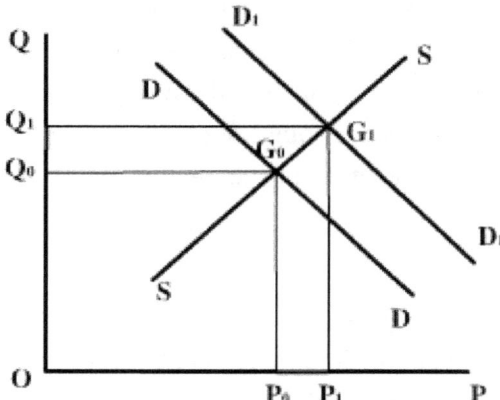

Figure 1.14: Short-term equilibrium market

Suppose that all people and enterprises think that the economy will develop strongly in the future because the country has just joined in WTO. Although current income is like as before, everyone is joyful and happy when they think the economy of the country develops, it means the income in the future will increase and their purse is fuller. Everyone awards by themselves by increasing the expenditure from that time. Short-term line of total demand DD moves strongly to the right of the graph to the position D_1D_1 and short-term line of total supply SS is constant. Two new lines of total supply and total demand intersect at point G_1, correlative to average price $P_1 > P_0$ and yield $Q_1 > Q_0$. New short-term equilibrium state of the market is established at the level which the price and yield increase comparing with old equilibrium state, reflecting the excitement of all society before deciding to join in WTO of a nation.

Medium-term equilibrium

Suppose that the economy is at medium-term equilibrium state supposed with line of total demand DD and line of total supply SS intersecting at point G_0, correlative to average price P_0 and equilibrium yield Q_0 as in figure 1.15. As above we find the reaction of the market in short-term before the decision of joining in WTO of a country. However, in medium-term and long-term, the matter will be different when initial excited psychology is replaced by economic selections in the production and consumption. When joining in WTO, customs barrier must reduce and competitive pressure for domestic enterprises increases. Import duty of commodity and service reduces strongly, create the advantage for domestic sector of production because the input expense reduces. Therefore, medium-term line of total supply SS will shift to the left to the new position S_2S_2 as in figure. When join in WTO both of export and import increase, if internal economy has weak competition ability, the import increases more quickly than the export and vice versa. Therefore, after join in WTO, total demand and domestic commodity depend on competitive ability of the country in the world market. Suppose that domestic commodity proves weaker than in international competition, then total demand for domestic commodity reduces, medium-term total demand line DD shifts to the left to the position D_2D_2 on the graph.

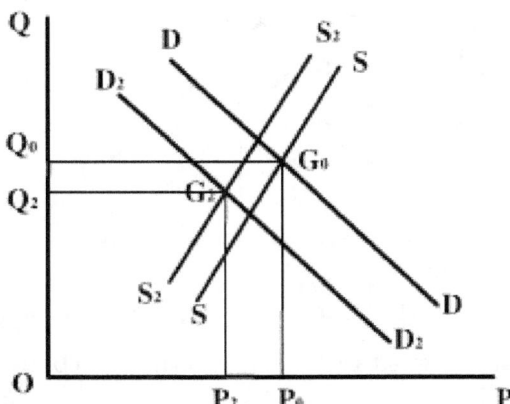

Figure 1.15: Medium-term equilibrium market

Two new medium-term lines of total supply and total demand (S_2S_2 & D_2D_2) intersect at point G2 correlative to average price $P_2 < P_0$ and $Q_2 < Q_0$. We find that in new equilibrium state, both of price and yield reduce, reflecting the weak competition of the economy of a country after joining WTO.

Long-term equilibrium

In section 1.7 we know that, the average rate of return of business block in long-term R_{DN} is equal to arithmetic average of long-term input and output interest rate of the bank system. In section 1.8 we judge that, the value of commodity is determined through expense of business operation and the average rate of return R_{DN}. Therefore, when considering entire economy in long-term, general average price P_0 of every commodity and service will be equivalent to general average value V_0 of every commodity and service.

Suppose that the economy is in long-term equilibrium state expected total demand line DD and total supply line SS intersecting at point G_0, correlative to average price $P_0 = V_0$ and equilibrium yield Q_0 as in figure 1.16.

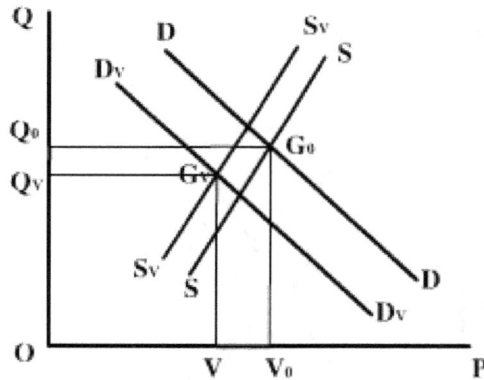

Figure 1.16: Long-term equilibrium market

We have just surveyed the medium-term equilibrium state of the economy with suppositions including the event of joining WTO and weak competitive ability of domestic economy comparing with the rest of the world. With such initial suppositions, long-term lines of total supply and total demand of the economy will shift to the direction similar to medium-term lines of total supply and total demand. Total supply line SS moves to the position S_vS_v and total demand line DD moves to the position D_vD_v. These two new lines of total supply and total demand intersect at equilibrium point G_v correlative to general

Market Economy & Policy On Two Domestic Currencies

average price $P_v = V$ and the yield Q_v. V is long-term general average value of every commodity and service considered in new background of the economy. In this case, $V < V_0$, reflects that the expense of business operation of business block reduces when the country joins in WTO. And $Q_v < Q_0$ shows the weak competition of domestic economy when integrating in international economy.

The market economy has ability of adjusting by itself not only for an "WTO event" as supposed above but also for any shock according to other direction such as reducing the demand or increasing, reducing the supply. However, necessary adjustment time for markets, including markets of commodity and currency, back to equilibrium state depends on "intensity" of shocks. In reality, the financial crises or real estate market crises often produce a strong stir on entire economy and if let the market be self-adjusting, it takes much time and opportunity cost, Governments often intervene through policies of fiscal year – currency to limit the maximum damages caused by the economic crisis.

Chapter 2
KNOTS IN THE ECONOMY

The market economy operates on basis of natural competitive laws, suitable for inherent nature of people, so it brings the high effect and contributes in the development of the human. Laws on economic benefit equilibrium help the society allocate the scarce resources according to the method which is simple and little waste. However, many people oppose, they don't think like this! How do we explain when many people eat poorly to be able to get by, besides that expensive automobile assembly factories appear continuously. Is "left side" of market mechanism big? Where is the reasonableness of allocating the economic resources? The market mechanism operates on basis of personal benefits and observes the call of the currency. Many expensive automobile factories appear because many people are ready to buy them. The amount of money is very big but it originates from income, in other words, they make assets for the society and enjoy the corresponding achievements, they don't take from the purse of other people! And how are poor people? They don't have money to buy food, in full words, they produce too few assets to exchange the food for keeping alive themselves. Therefore, is the market mechanism lucid, and is above whimsical situation the matter under humanitarian nature of people, is it beyond the economic relation? However, unemployment and bankruptcy are right products of market mechanism; severe competition will lead to such result. Equitably, competition brings both of good and bad things; because of competition the human makes progress. Nowadays, the economy of countries is better, science and technology have great strides, but there are still sudden natural calamities out of ability of confronting of human or peculiar diseases of mass murder. Clearly, people must make much progress to meet the requirements from objective reality. The competitive mechanism, although having side-effect, is necessary to impulse the development of the human.

In this chapter, we don't find the "bad habits" of the market economy, but try to show as many "knots" as possible in the economy. These are difficult problems or "abatis" on the way of economic development. Several in economic knots mentioned originates from the market mechanism, the rest originates from objective factors, out of the economy.

2.1 Growth model 0%

The economic growth is one of several important quotas of each country, measured by rate of yearly gross domestic product (GDP). Data quoted in Table 2.1 shows the speed of growth of GDP of some developed countries.

The growth of GDP in some developed countries (% year)						
Year \ Country	Canada	US	Japan	Britain	France	German
2000	5.29	3.69	2.84	3.78	3.79	2.86
2001	1.78	0.76	0.20	2.30	2.05	1.19
2002	2.94	1.61	0.26	2.06	1.03	0.00
2003	1.82	2.52	1.41	2.67	1.09	-0.19
2004	3.30	3.92	2.74	3.26	2.47	1.25
2005	2.94	3.23	1.91	1.93	1.71	0.91
2006	2.80	2.90	2.20	2.76	1.99	2.77

Table 2.1: Growth rate of GDP of some developed countries in years from 2000 – 2006. Resource: General Statistics Office of Vietnam and www.worldbank.org.

In developing countries, speed of economic growth is higher than developed countries. Table 2.2 shows the rate of GDP of Vietnam and some developing countries in stage 2000-2006.

Growth rate of GDP of some developing countries (% year)							
Year	Country	Vietnam	Thailand	Indonesia	China	India	Brazil
2000		6.79	4.75	4.92	8.00	3.94	4.40
2001		6.89	2.17	3.83	8.30	5.28	1.31
2002		7.08	5.32	4.50	9.10	3.73	2.61
2003		7.34	7.14	4.78	10.00	8.39	1.27
2004		7.79	6.28	5.03	10.10	8.33	5.72
2005		8.44	4.49	5.68	10.40	9.23	2.90
2006		8.23	5.02	5.48	10.70	9.20	3.72

Table 2.2: Growth rate of GDP of some developing countries in years from 2000 – 2006. Resource: General Statistics Office of Vietnam and www.worldbank.org.

The economic growth increases the resource in the society, and when the rate of economic growth is bigger than the rate of increasing population, the income per person also increases, enriching the physical life and moral life of each person. The growth model 0% is not the desire of countries; that is the warning which can happen in developed countries in some certain conditions. The final part of this section will present about that bad risk, however firstly we must have the basic information on method of accounting GDP and considering the function of economic growth.

2.1.1 Gross domestic product (GDP)

Gross domestic product (GDP) measures the yield of commodity and service produced by domestic and abroad enterprises, locating around the country, in a year.

The process of commodity production must spend many intermediate stages; therefore, to account exactly GDP, we add only value added part at each stage of business operation. The result shows that GDP is equal to total final commodity yield produced by domestic economy in a year. So, we have two methods of calculating GDP and the answer must be identical. First method is to add all items of value added in the enterprises, it is equal to earnings before tax of production factors including labor and capital. Second method, used more usually, is to calculate total value of all final commodity and service made by the economy; it is equal to total expenditure of three groups: expenditure of households; expenditure for the investment of the enterprise and expenditure of the Government. With an open economy, because of trade relations among countries must summarize items of export and import to account fully into GDP.

It is necessary distinguish the nominal GDP and actual GDP. The nominal GDP accounts according to current price, and actual GDP accounts according to original price of a fixed year to eliminate the inflation which reduces the purchasing power of currency according to the time.

If designate Y as value of GDP, C as the expenditure of households, I as the expenditure for the investment in enterprises, G as the expenditure of the Government, NX as net export (NX is the result by subtracting import value from export value), we have the formula as following:

$$Y = C + I + G + NX \qquad (2.1)$$

The expenditure of households (C) includes the expenditure for daily activities, buying the durable commodity; enjoying the services of culture, tourism, healthcare,…; repairing house and buying new house.

Investment (I) includes expenditures of business company to build more factories, buy or rent more the working office, buy new machines, equipment or increase the reserve.

The expenditure of Government (G) including the expenditure of the central government and local government, is divided into many items such as: buy equipment for administrative work, build the head office, buy equipment for work of national defense – security; large the roads, bridges, hospital, school and other public works.

Net export (NX) is calculated by subtract total import value from total export value.

Besides determining GDP, the economists bring out other values to evaluate the income scale of each country and person.

Gross national product (GNP) of a country is the economic yield made by the production factors originated from the country, not depend on place of production.

GNP = GDP + income from foreign country of domestic factors – income of factor of foreign country in the country.

Net national product (NNP) is the rest of GNP after eliminating depreciations related to capital.

NNP = GNP – depreciation related to capital under GNP

After calculating GDP, GNP, NNP, these values divided by gross domestic people will make correlative values per person.

2.1.2 Function of economic growth

We know that, besides the method of determining GDP according to method of accumulating the expenditures on buying final commodity, we can calculate GDP by accounting the production factors according to income.

Call L volume of labor in entire economy, W average salary before tax of each laborer, we have total salary value WL.

Call K total investment capital in entire economy, R as average salary before tax of an investment capital unit, we have total income of investment capital as RK.

So, we can definite GDP according to other method, according to the formula:

$$GDP = Y = WL + RL \qquad (2.2)$$

Look at equation 2.2 we find the yield Y depends on two input factors as labor (L) and investment (K). When production factors change, for example labor volume changes or investment capital changes, then Y also changes. Besides that people find that, technology progress increases the labor productivity and effect of investment capital. Therefore, yield Y is a function depending on three factors: labor volume, total investment capital and technology progress.

$$Y = A.F(K,L) \qquad (2.3)$$

In which A is general productivity of production factors, reflecting the level of technology at present.

From the equation 2.3, economists base on analyzing economy and changing mathematics to infer **function of growth** having following form:

$$\frac{\Delta Y}{Y} = \alpha \frac{\Delta K}{K} + (1-\alpha) \frac{\Delta L}{L} + \frac{\Delta A}{A} \qquad (2.4)$$

In which:

$\Delta Y/Y$ is rate of economic growth

$\Delta K/K$ is rate of increasing investment capital

$\Delta L/L$ is rate of increasing labor volume

α is contribution rate of capital factor in economic yield ($0 > \alpha < 1$)

$(1-\alpha)$ is contribution rate of labor factor in economic yield

$\Delta A/A$ is rate of increasing general productivity of production factor

We refer to following statistic table 2.3 to find the contribution rate of production factors and general productivity in growth on GDP of United States in the period from 1950 – 1999.

Contribution rate of production factors and general productivity in growth of United States economy (%/year)				
Period	Growth resources			
	Yield	Capital	Labor	Productivity
	ΔY/Y = α. ΔK/K + (1-α). ΔL/L + ΔA/A			
1950-1999	3.6	1.2	1.3	1.1
1950-1960	3.3	1.0	1.0	1.3
1960-1970	4.4	1.4	1.2	1.8
1970-1980	3.6	1.4	1.2	1.0
1980-1990	3.4	1.2	1.6	0.6
1990-1999	3.7	1.2	1.6	0.9

Table 2.3: Contribution rate of production factors and general productivity in growth of United States economy (%/year). Resource: Lecture on macroeconomics - Nguyen van Ngoc, National Economics University Publishing House, Hanoi, 2008

2.1.3 Growth model 0%

Now, we learn in details about three factors affecting rate of economic growth.

Rate of increasing laborer volume (ΔL/L)

When the economy develops stably, rate of unemployment is at low level, called natural unemployment level. In short-term periods, the economy can change up and down, change the rate of unemployment around natural unemployment level. In long-term, volume of laborers having job depends on manpower resource, and manpower resource depends on rate of increasing population. In some developing countries with rate of increasing population quickly in previous years, yearly labor resource increases strongly at present because there are many people starting to join in labor force, number of retired people is fewer.

Therefore, these countries have conditions to expand investment, attract more work to create many products for the society, contributing in the economic growth. In the long term, the population can't increase forever, but have to stabilize the scale at suitable level because the land and resources is limited, so the growth way based on labor scale is not firm. In the other hand, the growth based on population scale doesn't increase the yield per person so not raise the life quality.

In some developing countries, from many past years the rate of increasing population is very low and in some places having the tendency of reducing, yearly manpower resource increases hardly on scale. Therefore, a number of people who need to find the job increases yearly equivalent to number of laborers reaching to retired age, so real labor volume working in the economy increases insignificantly. Then $\Delta L/L \approx 0$.

Rate of increasing investment capital ($\Delta K/K$)

Data in table 2.3 shows that contribution in the economic growth of two factors labor and investment capital is equivalent. Normally, investment capital and number of labor having the job change in the same direction, the investment capital increases, number of labor increases and vice versa. Therefore, countries with plentiful labor resource are convenient in attracting the investment capital of enterprises at home as well as abroad.

In places where the labor resource doesn't increase, the investment capital is hard to increase or increase slowly according to the time. Therefore, if $\Delta L/L \approx 0$ then $\Delta K/K \approx 0$.

Rate of increasing general productivity of production factors ($\Delta A/A$)

General labor productivity of production factors (A) reflects current technology level of production force. Value A depends on quality of manpower resource and progress level of labor tools using in the economy. The quality of manpower resource shows in the following aspects: labor skill, initiative of improving the product quality, creativeness for new products. The progress level of labor tools shows in the productivity of machines and equipment, stability of product quality, expense for operating machines and equipment.

In developing countries, the technology level of production force is rather backward comparing with high-developed countries. Therefore, countries in third world have good conditions to raise the technology level through attracting the investment from advanced countries, strengthen the technology transfer, training association to raise the quality of manpower resource. So, labor productivity in developing countries has the high-growth potentiality, rate of increasing general productivity of production factors ($\Delta A/A$) in developing countries is rather attractive.

With high-developed countries, the situation is not simple as developing countries. Because of technology level under leading group of the world, advanced countries want to improve production technology; they can rely on only themselves. They must raise the quality of manpower resource, promote the creativeness to improve the production technology steps by steps, through that increase general productivity of input factors ($\Delta A/A$). Therefore, the hope for technology progress and labor productivity in developed countries put on the shoulders of the education department and investment resource for research field of the state as well as private individuals.

We find that, the knowledge about science and technology of human is very big, and to invent technology or continue improving the technology, current scientists must overpass the existing huge knowledge volume. According to the time, the leading scientists nowadays must overpass not only themselves but also the creative fence of human in the past. Meanwhile, archaeologists find that the brain of human has stable size from tens thousand years. The longevity of the human increases but slower than the progress of technology science, so everyone doesn't have much time to accumulate the knowledge and pursue their dream. After 25 years old, the brain stops developing and can reduce number of nervous cell. Raising the nutrition regime and physical practice can help cheery spirit, contributing in increasing the labor productivity but can't create sudden mutation in the thought. Therefore, a competence without expected can happen, at some moment, the creative ability of human doesn't increase or increase slowly. Then the technology level also makes no progress and general productivity of production factors changes insignificantly.

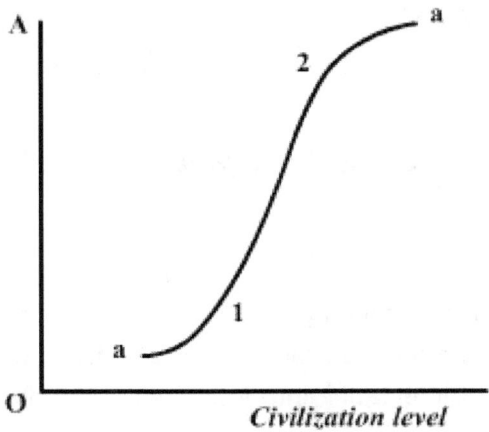

Figure 2.1: Productivity changes according to progress of civilization

In figure 2.1, the curve line aa reflects the change of general productivity A in direction of progress of human civilization, At first stage of the civilization, from ancient times to end of feudal regime, labor productivity and technology level increase very slowly according to the time, this stage is showed by section a-1 in the graph. When human civilization changes from feudal regime to capitalism regime, labor productivity and technology science develop as rain-storm, this stage starts from after position 1 in the graph. Nobody knows exactly where the final point of this stage is, but can only predict by feeling. Perhaps the most quickly developing stage of technology science finished in 2000, it means position 2 in the graph. The graph part after position 2 is from century XXI and after. If the prediction is exact, developed countries are at the stage in which labor productivity and technology progress increase slowly, it means it still increases but more slowly with previous stage.

If some developed countries have general productivity A increasing insignificantly, it means ΔA/A ≈ 0, plus the situation of constant manpower resource and investment capital (ΔL/L ≈ 0, ΔK/K ≈ 0) in those places, hardly there is economic growth. We have the final result by filling the number into the formula 2.4:

ΔY/Y = α. ΔK/K + (1-α). ΔL/L + ΔA/A ≈ 0.

This is a form of expression of growth model 0%.

2.2 Contradiction between production and consumption

In the market economy, there is division of labor and high specialized production, the production and consumption are apart. The larger process of integrating into international economy is, the higher specialized production is. Large market scale is the change and challenge for each enterprise. Nowadays, most of countries joined into WTO and customs fence is lowered, creates equal competitive environment but more fierce among countries as well as enterprises.

Production and consumption are two big economic categories, impacting each other, both unification and contradiction. In most of time, manufacturers – represent for seller and consumption households – represent for buyer often find the common voice in the market, through that contributing in stabilizing macroeconomics. Contradiction between production and consumption, although not happen regularly, leaves the serious consequence. Contradiction in small scale leads to unemployment and local bankruptcy, contradiction in big scale surely causes the economic crisis. There are many reasons which have the danger of causing conflict between production and consumption, we learn about hereafter.

2.2.1 False prediction

In the middle of the year 2008, when crude oil price was over 100 USD/barrel, many investment banks predicted that the price of oil in 2009 could be over 200 USD/barrel. After that the price of oil increased at high level 147 USD/barrel in the middle of July 2008. Since that the price of oil nosedived, at the beginning of December 2008 the price was one-third of peak period in July. Before the meeting of OPEC block dated December 16th 2008, the price of oil was over 40 USD/barrel, investors in the commodity market predicted that this block would reduce yield strongly and push the price of oil up to level 50 USD/barrel. In the meeting dated December 16th 2008, OPEC block agreed to reduce the yield 2 million barrels/day in total yield 27 million barrels/day. Besides that, Russia, a country having big oil yield but out of OPEC block, also agreed to reduce the yield about 400 thousand barrels/day with the hope of raising the oil price. With reducing such big oil yield, normally the oil price must increase, but in reality, it reduced rather strongly right after decisions on reducing were informed, down to 37 USD/barrel – the lowest price from before 4 years.

Refer to the predictions in Vietnamese securities market, there are interesting things. Not including predictions of domestic securities companies, only follow analysis sheet of HSBC, a big and famous bank in the world, we can infer the conclusion. In the middle of the year 2007, when securities index in the floor of Hochiminh City was around level of 1000 points, HSBC predicted VN-INDEX at the end of the year 2007 was about 900 points and at the end of the year 2008 was 1100 points. At the end of the year 2007, VN-INDEX stopped at level of over 900 points, so the prediction of HSBC firstly was exact. In quarter 1 of 2008, HSBC still thought that at the end of the year 2008 VN-INDEX reached 1100 points. But in quarter 2 of 2008, in the background of anti-inflation, Vietnamese government executed to tighten the currency, the report of HSBC on Vietnamese securities market had big change, they thought that VN-INDEX at the end of the year 2008 was at level of 600 points, reducing near a half of previous predictions, amazing in investment field. In quarter 3 of 2008, while VN-INDEX was around level of 500 points, in analysis sheet on Vietnamese market, HSBC thought that at the end of the year 2008, VN-INDEX was only about 400 points.

Another prediction at government level in 2008 damaged significantly for farmers, later Minister of Agriculture and Rural Development admitted the responsibility before the National Assembly, this is an example for reference. At the beginning of the year 2008, the price of rice in the world started to increase and at the end of quarter 1 of 2008 rose up to 1000 USD/ton, it meant to double the moment at the beginning of the year. Vietnam and Thailand were "powerful countries" on exporting rice, so the rice price in the world increasing highly would be advantage for agriculture. In the stage the rice price in the world increased highly, the price in the country also increased strongly because businessmen strengthened to buy rice in order to export and earn interest. The domestic rice price increasing highly increased inflation index, worried the Government. In the world market, rice price continued increasing and reached the top 1200USD/ton at the beginning of quarter 2 of 2008. At the time, Vietnamese Government decided to stop exporting rice because worrying the domestic rice price to increase strongly and not good prediction on the result of next rice crop which can affect national food security. After raising the peak level of 1200USD/ton, the rice price in the world started to reduce because many places in the world had good crops of cereals at the beginning of the year. In our country, contrary to the government's predictions, in crop of spring-summer 2008, the farmers had good crop everywhere from North to South. At this moment, if re-connecting the decision on exporting rice, it was too late because rice price reduced strongly, remaining a half of peak period.

Above examples don't aim at assessing the ability of true - false prediction of organizations or individuals, but say that the prediction is very difficult and has high risk. However, the predictions are always input data for important decisions from macro-level to micro-level. The Governments must bring out the prediction on the inflation situation, consumption level of people and investment capital resource in entire society to have decision on policy of fiscal year and currency. The enterprises must depend on predictions on commodity demand, business situation of competitors as well as developments in the market to establish the plan of business operation. True prediction will lead to exact decisions, false prediction will lead to unfavorable decisions. Because the prediction has high risk, in many cases the policies of the Government makes negative impact to the economy. The enterprises often meet the complications because of superabundant production without consuming; perhaps they must close the factory or go bankrupt.

2.2.2 Change on climate and natural calamity

Have many warnings in science field on unstable future of global climate weather because people use too many energy causing pollution for life environment. Changes on climate and natural calamity can cause bad impact on many fields, especially agriculture. Flood, drought and storm cause bad harvest in many places in the world, create the shocks on supply resource of agricultural products causing market disorder. Unusual climate weather arises many kinds of epidemic diseases in crop plants and domestic animals, losing food hygiene safety leading to the fact consumers turn their back and finally bankrupting the breeding field. Earthquake, tsunami, storm can damage or destroy the infrastructure, big industrial works, resident areas... affecting entire economy.

2.2.3 War, terror and ethnic group contradiction

In the world there are many implicit contradictions which can lead to the war, terror and ethnic group contradiction. These are differences about political system, disputes on territory and sea area, competition on resources and minerals, religion and moral values. These sensitive problems affect the production, consumption and international trade relation. Unstable world increases the risks and limits the investment flow, affects negatively the belief on consumption of people everywhere, obstructs cultural exchange and tourism.

2.2.4 Price control alliance

Organization of Petroleum Exporting Countries (OPEC) is a typical example on price control alliance. Countries in OPEC block hold most of petroleum reserves in the world, while the petroleum is important input material of many branches of industry. By decisions on increasing or reducing the yield, OPEC can make oil price fluctuate continuously in the market. Under the control of OPEC, the oil price had ever triplicated in two years 1973-1974 and doubled in stage 1979-1980.

In the field of production or commodity distribution, in branches with few supply enterprises, can happen the phenomenon of colluding with each other to form the price control alliance to manipulate the market, distort the supply and the demand and limit the competitive ability in entire branch.

2.2.5 Consumption according to the movement

Formerly, Vietnam Television and some local televisions compete to project a mass of attractive full-length films of Korea, create the fan wave of Vietnamese people towards Kim chi country. From the fever on television to the fever in real life, people call for reach other and buy the fashion items according to Korean model such as clothes, cosmetics, shoes, hair style ... There is demand the there will be supply, importers will select many commodities from Korea, domestic manufacturers and service suppliers reproduce the imported model to attract the customers. Therefore, unusual consumption movement controls significantly the tendency of business operation.

People often have the habit of aping each other, firstly are a group of people, after that spread out and create the movement; that is phenomenon of crowd psychology.

Crowd psychology can create many tendencies on consumption and investment such as: movement of building house, movement of buying motorbike, movement of playing share... Consumption movements can deform the production, shift investment resource and when the consumption movement finishes, it will leave disastrous consequence for later enterprises.

Contrary to the consumption movement is "movement" of tightening the expenditure. Firstly people think that tightening the expenditure is an action of saving, well for the economy, but in reality it is not like this. If because the predictions with short of optimistic about the economy of the country, everyone tightens the expenditure together to prevent the risks and this can damage the economy. When everyone limits shopping, the sales turnover reduces strongly, leading to reduce the production and close a mass of factories, workers lose the jobs and have no income. So consumers, from taking the initiative in tightening the expenditure, become people who must tighten the expenditure. The consumption tendencies which are too excited or "contractive" according to crowd psychology often damage the economy and consumers; however, such actions according to style of "to be hoist with one's own petard" still exist popularly in the economy.

2.3 Cohabitation with inflation

Inflation is the phrase which is mentioned with high frequency on mass media and in social life. Inflation is understood in some various ways, but due to its universalness, we need to simplify concept of inflation so that it is convenient in communication and information exchange.

Inflation is the phenomenon of currency's purchasing power decline; inflation rate is determined by rate of consumption price index in one - year time.

In consideration of long-term development process, inflation has universal property in every economy from high developed countries to underdeveloped ones. Sometimes between two periods appear one period when commodity price goes down, that is the inflation period - it manifests a common price rate that decreases but not increase.

Table 2.4 is data about inflation rate of Vietnam from stage 2000 to 2007, calculated under index of CPI every year.

Inflation rate of Vietnam from stage 2000 to 2007 (% year)								
Year	2000	2001	2002	2003	2004	2005	2006	2007
inflation	-0.6	0.8	4.0	3.0	9.5	8.4	9.6	12.6

Table 2.4: Inflation rate of Vietnam from stage 2000 to w2007, calculated under index of CPI. Source: General Statistics Office of Vietnam.

To calculate consumption price index, General Statistics Office of Vietnam divides consumption goods and service into ten groups with weight of each group in direct ratio to sales figures. Each month, they collect data about consumption price on the market on in three days in equal distance to calculate average price of each type of goods. When in comparison with price rate between various periods, we can infer results of consumption price index under month, quarter or year.

Table 2.5 is data about inflation situation in several countries in the stage from 2000 to 2006, calculated under compared price of GDP every year.

Inflation rate in several countries (%year)					
Year	Countries	Thailand	Indonesia	Singapore	Korea
	2000	1.36	...	5.37	0.80
	2001	2.07	16.72	-1.80	3.50
	2002	0.80	3.68	-1.22	2.80
	2003	1.37	5.45	-1.03	2.72
	2004	3.22	8.54	3.75	2.74
	2005	4.50	14.80	0.30	-0.26
	2006	5.00	13.64	0.20	-0.26

Table 2.5: inflation rate in several Asian counties from 2000 to 2006, calculated under compared price of GDP. Source: Calculated based on data of General Statistics Office of Vietnam.

2.3.1 Basic inflation index

Common inflation rate measures price fluctuation of all consumption service and commodity groups, in our country there are ten groups of commodity, called general inflation index. Beside general inflation rate, economists also establish other inflation index, called basic inflation index. Basic inflation index also defined the same as general inflation index but it is only different at quantity of consumption commodity groups for calculation. Goods basket to calculate basic inflation does include goods groups: foods - foodstuff and energy. When we eliminate two groups: foods - foodstuff and energy from the basic inflation index calculating basket, the weight of the remaining goods groups must be rationally changed.

Why do economists bring out basic inflation index?

We see that two consumption goods groups are rations – foodstuff and energy which are essential goods groups nearly used every day by each household. When price of commodity groups changes that also impacts much each household's quantity of expense. Each household's savings is often used to buy durable goods or repair a house, buy a new house. Socioeconomic organizations consign savings for use target of investment in the future. They do not save money to buy rations, meat, fish or petroleum in the future. Hence basically, fluctuation of rations - foodstuff or energy price does not profit or harm for depositors, because money saving target must not be to buy those goods. Therefore, depositors including families and economic organizations can consult from basic inflation index to see disadvantage and advantage level when they continue to keep money instead of present expenditure. If saving interest rate is bigger than basic inflation rate, saving at present and expenditure later will be more advantageous. Otherwise, when basic inflation rate is bigger than saving interest rate, present expenditure in general is more advantageous in comparison with the case of consigning money to spend later.

Hence all objects are interested in general inflation index; particularly persons with savings are also interested in basic inflation index. For credit agencies and central Bank, basic inflation index is sometimes more interested compared with general inflation index because it is a basis to form input interest platform at financial institutions.

2.3.2 Bad affects of inflation

Inflation makes currency devalue according to time so it influences money users as means of hoard. Although they are made up by interest rate but because unusualness of inflation makes money keepers' mind unsafe, they must always consider the advantage and disadvantage between immediate expenditure and saving continuity. Inflation develops unexpectedly which causes high risk to lending contracts and maturity payment. Banking operation has a considerable effect since capital flow is unstable and mainly short-term. Extended and large investment works and will be hiked price and difficult to make arrangement, construction contracts or equipment and machine, raw materials assessed availably will become backward and unable of feasibility that comes to deadlock for works.

In inflation background, price level of commodity changes according to time so business operation units regularly change quotation, restaurant and hotel amend price list in menu, commercial centers must spend more to change price list and type of advertising catalogue. Consumers spend time since they must regularly update market information to have decisions on rational expenditure. Inflation makes laborer's actual revenue decline though nominal salary level still preserves, so it can create contradiction among employees and employers, once salary level is not properly adjusted with market price fluctuation.

Inflation creates a favorable condition for venture operation. Venture capital flow at first only focuses on some commodities with sensitive fluctuation price level that turns items become scarce, artificial and increase strongly. In market economy, items are little related to each other, for example rice price increases other cereals sooner or later also raise or building materials increase that leads to real estate price increase, so when there is a sudden increase at several goods that immediately impacts other dependent and subsidiary goods. Chain price increase reaction begins to form in parallel with venture operation of price stimulation that turns market situation become confused. If psychographics is unstable but falls in state of panic, price level will boom and sales figures also accelerate. Bank's input interest is compelled to increase high to ensure liquidity, therefore input interest also raises that obstructs elementary and long-term investment, when price platform is at high rate, interest is extremely high, currency policy is tightened, psychographics goes down, and then venture spiral also ends. Its consequence left is a "battlefield" in confusion with "successes" and failures. Sharp businessmen earn crowded of money, the objects who participate late must "hug time bomb", consumers are also tired and exhausted of money. After the stage increases temporarily hot, there will be a costly and hard regulation stage of economy.

2.3.3. Cause for inflation

In each period of inflation, if we find out the cause exactly that increases price, anti-inflation will be quickly effective and less costly for economy.

Inflation due to currency

We have studied goods exchange equilibrium equation at the former chapter and it is very useful for inflationary cause analysis. The equation is written as follows:

$$PQ = MV$$

This equation always is correct in every survey interval

P is average price rate of types of goods – service (called commodity in common)

Q is sum of transacted commodity with payment

M is total face value of currency in circulation

V is a number of average circulations of currency unit

From the above equation, we infer a formula of average price level: $P = MV/Q$.

Q is total quantity of transacted commodity with payment, so if consider in long term, Q is depends on economic growth rate. Because when economy develops, commodity transaction also increases in direct ratio, and when economy stops, quantity of transacted commodity does not almost change. However, consider in short term when in comparison with months in year value of Q can change. For instance in Tet month, people spend much, so quantity of transacted commodity will be bigger compared with other months in year.

V is a number of average circulations of currency unit. V mainly depends on household's expenditure habit and enterprises' production circle. Besides, value of V depends on security level of banking system.

Market Economy & Policy On Two Domestic Currencies

Because when banking system meets issue, households and economic organizations want to hold more cash to prevent risk it delays currency circulation process. But in fact, almost all time banking system operates normally and safely so the public and enterprises only keep the amount of money properly to pay transaction under cycles, the remaining is transferred to savings deposits under maturity to enjoy interest. Hence in long term, V is relatively secure. Consider in short term, V can change under psychographics, when the public is enthusiastic to spend V will rise, V inversely reduces. But let's note that when V increases that will make Q increased, when V reduces that will make Q declined, so we see that V/Q does not almost change in short term. Particularly in case of insecurity of baking system, V decreases relatively strongly but Q reduces little, so at that time V/Q will go down.

M is total face value of circulation currency. Since banking operation is very diversified and complex, there appears much controversy about calculation of quantity of circulation currency. We list various currency norms and choose value for proper calculation.

Designation	List of assets directly under bank
M	Total issued cash outside central Bank
M0	Cash in circulation = M – reserve cash at commercial banking system
M1	M0 + non-maturity deposits + amount of deposits which can be written by payment cheque
M2	M1 + short-term savings deposits
M3	M2 + long-term savings deposits
M4	M3 + short-term bond + financial tools which are easy to transfer into cash

Table 2.6: Currency norms

We know that, in market economy, currency plays a role as means of payment and means of hoard. This part's target is to find out relation between inflation and volume of currency so let's concentrate on volume of standing currency in payment. M1 is volume of currency which needs to be interested. Long-term, short-term savings deposits or bond are amount of money in hoard, it has not yet been means of payment, though it can quickly convert into means of payment. Moreover, in the normal condition of economy, amount of money is converted from hoard currency into circulation currency; similarly there is volume of currency converting from circulation to hoard currency.

If other conditions are secure, M1 will increase when central Bank pumps more amount of new cash into the market (i.e., increase supply of M). M1 also rises when banking system operates safely and effectively. In case commercial banking system losses prestige, the public will hold more cash (i.e., M0 increases), then if M does not change, reserves in banking system remain very little, payment activities through bank lead to reducing strongly, so it declines M1.

From equation $P = MV/Q$, we realize that, in long term V little changes, Q changes under economic growth rate so: if M1 increases in direct ratio to Q, level of prices of P will stable, if M1 raises more quickly than economic growth rate, P will go up and cause inflation.

In short term values of Q and V can change but they fluctuate in the same direction, quotient of V/Q does not nearly change. Hence average price of P still depends on change of total amount of M1.

Inflation due to demand

Consumption and investment activities are irregularly stable but also have a change under psychological factor. When belief in consumption increases, speed of money expenditure is more rapid that raises V and pushes Q increase. Investment operations take place more eventfully, demand of borrowing and lending rises and payment through bank accelerates that rises M1. When the real estate market, gold market or share market increase hot, it will increase assets value of a part of the public. Expectation of revenue increases which promotes expenditure at present and grows inflation. In special case, when consumption movement accelerates in combination with broad venture operation, weakness in flexibility in operation by Government maybe will kindle outbreak of price.

Inflation due to pushing expense

In the above parts, we have known lots reasons which cause one shock of supply including factors: climate, political contradiction or monopoly coalition of yield control. Some basic commodities increases price that can cause Domino effect which raises price of mass other commodities and finally creates inflation. For example: when price of mineral-oil rises that will raise direct price for output products of petrochemical industry as: petrol, polime materials, lubricant, gas, etc. Increase in these products will lead to putting up input expense for various economic sectors, of which transport branch is typical. Transport service also causes effect on the whole economic activities.

When in consideration of long-term process, we realize that the global population has not been a stable symbol about scale but still swells out, world economy is still a trend of increase, human demand is limitless. Besides land source, mineral resources are limited and are reducing everyday. This certainly creates contradiction among supply and demand that turns the price of raw materials and land lease have a tendency to going up according to time. Input raw materials will increase the price of almost all other items and cause inflation according to time.

2.4 Unemployment

Unemployment often happens in all nations where there is not any low or high development level discrimination, the mater we need to concern which level unemployment rate is and what losses it causes for society. Data in Table 2.7 total up unemployment in some nations in Asian area, the stage from 2000 to 2006.

Unemployment rate in some countries (% year)					
Year	Vietnam	Thailand	Indonesia	Singapore	Korea
2000	6.42	2.86	6.07	4.42	4.13
2001	6.28	2.91	8.10	3.44	4.08
2002	6.01	3.50	9.06	4.22	3.28
2003	5.78	3.03	9.56	4.49	3.56
2004	5.60	2.76	9.85	4.44	3.67
2005	5.31	2.42	11.24	4.22	3.73
2006	4.82	2.04	10.44	3.39	3.44

Table 2.7: Unemployment rate in Vietnam and some Asian countries in years from 2000 to 2006. Source: Calculated based on data of General Statistics Office of Vietnam

Unemployment rate reflects correlation between a number of people who are looking for jobs in total people under labor force.

Labor force includes people who are working and persons who under working age want to look for jobs.

Non – labor force concentrates on persons who have ability to work under working age, but due to private reason, not take part in labor force.

Human resources are persons who are able to work and are in working age. Human resources include labor force and non – labor force.

2.4.1 Reason for unemployment

In human social history there has ever had stage without unemployment. This is in Primitive Commune, the people live and work together, and they share to enjoy labor achievements. Former Socialist Republic nations do not also have unemployment, or to be exact unemployment happens little. Majority of people do not want return to those social regimes, because it is too backward or bureaucratic and sluggish, short of creativity and less effective. Market economy considers competition to motivate for development, and once it appears competition certainly it leads to mutual elimination and leaves consequences such as bankruptcy and unemployment.

Competition in the same sector continuously takes place, enterprises with high profit rate try to expand scale and enterprises, which work at a loss narrow production or wind up plant and this leads to provisional unemployment in some of laborers. The fact shows, when production scale of the whole sector does not change, a number of labors in the sector do not go down because several enterprises cut down jobs, the others inversely recruit more employees, and so there is not unemployment in the sector. However, because production field is too large and expresses global, the job lost persons and selected ones come from in various nations, consequently in this case it still causes unemployment at the place where there are dismissed laborers.

Contradiction between supply and demand happens regularly at level of production field or in the whole economy. Plans for business operation in large scale against the market or a shock of supply or demand may create chain effects in the economy and cause mass unemployment. Overproduction in large scale is a reason for industrial crisis in years from 1929 to 1933; and the shocks of petroleum in decades of 1970 and 1980 of the former century also caused unemployment at two-number level in many countries. The contradiction between production and consumption in narrow scale is more popular and increases unemployment. For instance, bad oxen epidemic in England or melamine infected milk in China, all lead to the plight the oxen breeders were mass unemployment.

Regulations about minimum salary grade for laborers can increase unemployment if average salary grade is short of reality. In close economy, rationally minimum salary grade does not much influence unemployment, since all enterprises conform to the same rules. However, the close economy is different; each country has various minimum salary grades so it may cause inequality among enterprises in the same line but their production in different countries. Beside minimum salary barrier, inflexible regulations about salary in labor contract also contribute to intensifying unemployment. Goods price in the market fluctuates ceaselessly go up or down, while salary is a lack of flexibility, it certainly causes a difficulty for companies and sometimes they lead to narrowing production or become careful in receiving more laborers.

In addition, some people are self-motivated to integrate the unemployment staff for personal reasons. Many persons leave their company due to internal contradiction or unfit of "liking" with their leaders; the some initially work ardently but later not suit their strong point and decide to leave. Those objects all are voluntary to be temporarily unemployed and of course, this contributes to rising unemployment rate.

2.4.2 Bad affects due to unemployment

Unemployment despite of any reason also causes waste of resources, reduces economic growth and social welfare. In the economy, unemployment is indispensable, however, if unemployment rate is low society can accept, but if it is at high rate and lengthens in lots of years, it gets stressful, just like a timer bomb. One part of laborers is in long – term unemployment, they lead to losing their income, and it causes difficulty in daily activities. Unemployment causes stress, inhibit the mind and sometimes develop contradiction in the family. Social evils arise due to a part of unemployment. Unemployment in large scale can cause disorder of social life, public disorder, ethnic contradiction, class contradiction and political crisis.

Nowadays many nations in over the world have unemployment benefit in some fixed months so that unemployed can have more income and have enough time to look for a new job. However, this is the only provisional solution, because the important matter is that whether economy is able to create more jobs so that unemployed can look for a job before expiring unemployment benefit.

2.4.3 Solutions for unemployment reduction

Market Economy & Policy On Two Domestic Currencies

Efforts from all ways aiming at to reduce unemployment are welcome by society. Long and strategic solution must be in training and education policy. Education branch needs to improve lecturing programs and education methods aiming at to train persons who are healthy, intelligent, active and creative, easily adjusted to economy's competitive environment. Education socialization is a rational choice aiming at to uphold all social resources for human upbringing work – a lofty cause but full of difficulty and costliness. The State needs to have assistance policies for the areas where there are many residents meeting difficulty, object with special plight, aiming at to generalize education broadly and improve space of People's cultural standard. University education and vocational education must follow closely reality aiming at to supply enough human resources under each line and enhance training quality by combination between theory and practice. For levels from middle level over, it is necessary to have test questions to help candidates choose lines properly with their health, intelligence, aptitude and character, ensure that candidates leave school, they will love their occupation and contribute more to society.

We need to have a really good combination mechanism among enterprises, job promotion centers, universities, vocational training centers and laborers to supply multidimensional information about demand of human resources, labor supply capacity, salary regime, etc aiming at to establish an effective and sound, open labor market. The action is very meaningful, it helps unemployed quickly approach labor market to look for new jobs or make up more knowledge so that they change to work in other fields.

Macroeconomic policy also makes an important contribution to unemployment reduction. Increase in unemployment often accompanies with inflation and economic yield decrease, so economic demand stimulation through policy on currency relaxation and Government's expenditure raise brings rapid and high result.

Contradiction between labor union and steering committee can cause stress in enterprises. It affects product quality, productivity and competitive capacity of enterprises, in many cases it comes to standstill of production and leading to unemployment. Need to build friendly relation between employers and labor union. Parties should have regular dialogue listen to their opinions, avoid objectively casual action from each party, restrict all capability that can create enterprise' internal contradiction.

2.5 Debt burden

Debt is the relatively popular phenomenon in individual ownership regimes. Like other phenomena, it is positive and negative. Based on borrowing and lending mechanism, capital flow shifts from redundant place to short one that helps equilibrate currency market, save resources in society. However, once debt is excessive and short of safety, it conceals a risk of chain crash that collapses the economy.

2.5.1 Two modes of main borrowing

Each family has a vital affair in need of spending a big amount, so they must save money in the long time to implement proposed targets, for example buying house, purchasing car. All those require families to save and accumulate in ten years, and then they can implement their targets. In the time of monetary accumulation, they can temporarily lend the accumulated amount and withdraw it when in need of expenditure. Some other families have a great affair in need of urgent expenditure but their accumulation is not enough, they want to borrow more amounts to implement the affair and will gradually pay the debt later. Business operation enterprises do the same; they all have investment plans according to time so some enterprises need to accumulate money and the others need to raise capital to carry out their investment project early. There is supply and demand of capital and it will indispensably form capital market where both lender and borrower satisfy the demand set up.

Bank credit

Banking system is the important part of capital market, having branches and dealing office rising all over living areas in the whole country. Bank supplies many services related to economic activities, but we here are only interested in credit service. Bank plays a role as the intermediary to combine lenders and borrowers. Lenders include individuals, households and socioeconomic organizations with temporarily redundant monetary resources, borrowers are enterprises that need invested capital for projects or individuals, households need money to pay great expenditure. Since inflation takes place every year, to equilibrate interest among parties and help credit market operate stably, bank needs to receive the interest from borrowers and pay interest for depositors. Banks rely on their prestige and Government's guarantee to establish trust for depositors, so that they can set their mind at rest to transfer a part of their assets to banks without mortgage. Borrowers cannot only expect individual's or enterprise's prestige to borrow but they need to have the mortgaged assets under Bank's regulations; then they can approach borrowed funds, this caution makes a contribution to increasing safety and effectiveness in credit activities.

Bond issue

Bond issue is a mode of loan, but it is established directly among borrowing party and lending one, not like bank credit activities. Bond issue objects can be Government or organs directly under Government, local authorities, large enterprises. Depending on issue objects, whose bonds have various names such as Governmental bond, State treasury paper, local authority bond and enterprise bond. Bond issue Government and organs directly under Government as well as local authority are based on their prestige, and enterprises, to issue bond need Governmental organs' guarantee and prestigious commercial banks' one. Bond has various types of maturity and bond creditors all are enjoyed interest, interest rate depends on each type of bond, issue time and moment. If it is the same time and moment of issue, Governmental bond has the lowest interest rate but enterprise bond is at higher interest rate. Bond purchasers include various compositions from individuals, households to socioeconomic organizations.

Consigning savings and purchasing bond have different and similar points. They are similar because they all are tools to serve hoard of money, have relatively high safety and are enjoyed rational interest. However, among them there are some differences, if consign savings you can draw it before maturity when there is an unexpected matter and you will enjoy lower interest, but buy bond you can not pay before maturity, bond must inversely be transacted again so instead of paying before maturity, you can sell it for other people in need.

2.5.2 Debt scale in economy

As we see the above, lending and borrowing activities originate from extremely natural demand of human in economic life. Debt is the normal affair in economic activities, but the bigger debt scale is certainly, it conceals a risk in lending activities and can have a bad impact on overall economic activities.

Debt in economy can divided into two big items: Government's debt and private enterprise's debt

Government's debt

When receipts from budget are not enough to spend, Governments often borrow by bond issue to sponsor excessive expenditures. Government Bond participants include external and internal organizations, individuals. Every year Government must pay bond interest for bond creditors and pay original part for expired bond blocks. Government's debt includes local and central authorities' unpaid loans accumulated from many years. Government borrows to implement national projects as: investment in infrastructure including road bridge, wharf or electric plant, or investment and improvement of school, hospital, scientific researches bases, even including expenditure on social security work. Government invests strongly in material facilities and human aiming at to promote economic development, create more jobs, improve social life, through that he intensify revenue sources to pay debts.

Debt in private enterprise block

Enterprises raise fund from credit channel or through bond issue to invest in effective business operation projects, or supplement capital resources for business operation. Enterprises hope the extension of business operation will raise more profits to make up for expenses and service of debt from creditors.

Individuals and households can also borrow money from credit agencies to buy durable goods and then deduct a part from monthly incomes to pay the debt under maturity.

In year 2007, according to State Bank's statistics, total credit balance of the whole banking system is about over one million billion dong (95% GDP). In our country, bond issue from enterprises is not favorable, so only few enterprises issue bond to mobilize capital but it is mainly the funding through credit channel. Hence, in year 2007, total debt in private enterprises in the whole country, including credit debt and bond issue debt is the equal rate of 100% GDP.

The trend of debt increase

Poor and rich gap in society is an important reason that increases debt. Persons with redundant assets and capital will use to invest or lend, and poor persons with low living standards are needful to borrow money to stabilize their life or improve their physical and spiritual life. Poor and rich gap has trend to increase, one reason is due to unequal inheritance, and the other is due to the gap about personal labor capacity that leads to too large difference in yearly income. In addition, marriage trend also contributes to poor and rich increase. Although it is not all and there is not any specific regulation, persons normally get married under rank. It means well-off persons come to together and the poor comes and lives altogether. Therefore, revenue division figure naturally is not the same color, now is colored more strongly due to marriage. Hence assets accumulation process through inheritance, difference about revenue and marriage trend is basic reasons that raise poverty and richness gap in society. In fact, Governments imposed individual income tax under progressive method to reduce inequality about income among resident classes. However, if tax rate rises too highly, it will reduce working motivation of talent persons whom any society also need use at an important function.

In world economic integration, it creates an increasing competitive pressure; this trend is favorable for large-scale enterprises but causes difficulty for small-scale enterprises or newly established ones. In broader and deeper integration world, share market also fluctuates unexpectedly and has high risk. Therefore, there are objects that with available funds do not actively want to invest but come to bank - saving channel or invest in bond for safety. Passive investment trend in society, which increases, will raise debt in economy.

In long term, economic yield depends on total supply but in short term, it is decided by total demand. Since active investment has high risk, savings increases and reduces total demand. That will lead to decreasing economic yield and rising unemployment. To ensure economic growth performance and social security, Governments must broaden fiscal year policy and are ready to issue more bonds to intensify investment aiming at to stimulate demand for economy. Government's debt consequently has trend of increase. Large-scale enterprises that work effectively and want to expand business operation scale and come to bank or issue bond to borrow capital. Hence, more and more debt in private-enterprise block swells out.

2.5.3 Economic risk due to debt

In condition when economy develops securely, debts seem not to influence much economic activities and social life. Then past-due accounts are under the control, interest and original debt at term all are fully paid, credit resources are relatively abundant that increases liquidity in economy. However, market economy itself conceals much insecurity and when that happens, the debt becomes serious and raises economic troubles. Weak macroeconomic indexes always accompany with bad debt increase and debt below standard in private enterprise sector. Then belief in economy declines and credit activities meet difficulty, economy becomes weak in liquidity. Investment resources reduce strongly, belief in consumption goes down, and it brings cut spiral of economic yield reduction and unemployment increase. The bigger the debt scale is, the stronger negative impact becomes and can cause economic crisis.

Economic crisis in global scale, which we are seeing from year 2008, originates from loan activities on mortgage below standard in America. In the long time, interest by Dollar is at low rate so American banks bravely lend all poor objects. They borrow money to purchase a house and use the purchased house as mortgage for bank. Everybody also thinks housing can increase but not decline so borrowing and lending activities are safe. Financial institutions, who have balance due of large real estate loan also create a new product by packing the balance due, and then divide into securities, then issue on the market. Receipts from the new securities issue are poured into loan market of housing below standard. Real estate becomes too hot and begins a sign of danger since year 2007. Real estate's blister in America deflates that causes much impact on its economic sectors such as decrease economic yield and increase unemployment. Poor households who borrow money to buy houses are the first victims of unemployment. They do not have enough money to pay the debts and are obliged to give back the mortgaged house to bank. Housing price declines strongly that causes great loss to financial institutions that hold assets related to the mortgages below standard in America, while it includes many financial institutions in Europe and Asia. Because of worrying about economic risk of high increase in economic risk, global credit activities reduces that causes partial liquidity in some countries. Series of banks and financial institutions in American and other countries had to declare bankruptcy. Countries' Governments have poured out hundreds billion US Dollar to save financial system. Credit crisis below standard in America quickly has turned into the globally financial crisis. Share price in over the markets declines depress fully, add housing reduction that makes households' assets abase evidently and they are obliged to cut down investment and limit consumption. Total demand in the whole world goes down strongly, this is a direct reason leading to the globally economic crisis, which is considered the biggest within 70 last years and is affecting all nations and territories in the world.

Chapter 3
MACROECONOMIC REGULATION

In the first chapter, we have studied operation principles of market economy and only favor is that market economy itself, in normal conditions has possibility of self-regulating well and not need violent interference of "visible hand". It seems free market and price regulation has "enough wisdom" to guide what enterprises and consumers know to acquire minimum profit, through this so that they can distribute scarce resources in economy effectively.

In the second chapter, we realize there are many factors, which from inside and outside economy can influence free market strongly, deforming market and causing troubles for economy. In some cases, the troubles are too large and if let economy self-regulates; it spends much time and opportunity cost. Then Government needs to express their role through mechanism adjustment and fiscal year - currency policy aiming at to stabilize macroeconomy.

3.1 Except of macroeconomic regulation

To evaluate one country's macroeconomic situation, they usually inspect basic macroeconomic quotas including Growth rate of GDP, inflation rate, unemployment rate and overall payment balance of economy. Besides, they can be more interested in some other indexes as commercial balance, receipts and payment of budget, national debts, growth quality, etc. Table 3.1 synthesizes several basic macroeconomic quotas of developed countries.

Average employment, growth, inflation of several developed countries in stage from 1960 to 2004 (%/year)			
	Britain	America	Germany
Unemployment			
1960-1973	3	5	1
1973-1981	6	7	3
1981-1990	10	7	7
1990-2001	7	5	7
2001-2004	5	5	9
Growth of GDP			
1960-1973	3	4	5
1973-1981	1	2	2
1981-1990	3	3	2
1990-2001	2	3	3
2001-2004	2	3	2
Inflation			
1960-1973	5	3	3
1973-1981	15	9	5
1981-1990	6	5	3
1990-2001	3	3	3
2001-2004	2	2	2

Table 3.1: Average unemployment, growth, inflation of several countries in some various stages. Source: Economists: David Begg, Stanley Fischer, Rudiger Dornbusch; Statistics Publisher of Hanoi, 2008.

Due to lots of various reasons, in fact market economy falls in unstable state, once economy meets a breakdown it will express at basic macroeconomic quotas. In the months of early beginning of 2008, due to many reasons, which make consumption, price index (CPI) of Vietnam increase high that causes insecurity for macroeconomic. At that time Government proposes focus task is to control inflation to stabilize macroeconomy. After Government implements tight policy on currency and limits expenditure, interest has a sign of high increase and investment projects by State-owned capital stops temporally. Since from July onwards, CPI has increased slightly and event reduced at three months of the end of the year (see data at Table 3.2)

Rate of CPI every month in Vietnam in 2008						
Month	1	2	3	4	5	6
CPI(%)	2.38	3.56	2.99	2.20	3.91	2.14
Month	7	8	9	10	11	12
CPI(%)	1.13	1.56	0.18	-0.18	-0.76	-0.68

Table 3.2: Growth rate of CPI every month in Vietnam in 2008, Source: General Statistics Office of Vietnam

Macroeconomic regulation is the affair which Government undertakes mechanism and conformable policy aiming at to optimize macroeconomic quotas.

To operate economy well, there must have positive participation of machinery of the State. On the one hand, functional organs must regularly improve market economy system to create a favorable condition for business and consumption operation. On the other hand, the Government needs to execute financial and monetary policy properly, depending on each specific situation, to assist economy develop soundly.

3.2 Market economy setups

Each model of economy has legal scope of distinct operation. Economic operation rules in the Feudal cannot apply into capitalist economy. Commodity economy has developed rather long-standing in human history, but due to many former restrictions about information, transport, etc, markets have not been established clearly but only existed in beginning, tattered form. Nowadays it is completely different, commodity markets and service increase strongly, rising outside the territory. Decisions about enterprises' production or each family's consumption choice cannot depend on subjective opinion but completely depending on market. Prosperity of one business field or regression of the other all is decided by the market. Government's policy cannot be arbitrary but must comply closely with market development. All those require each nation with economy in movement to market mechanism to need to build an appropriate economic system, form legal scope for markets to operate effectively.

Market economy system is a legal scope to operate market economy; including law regulation, behavior principles related to all participants in economy; be built under favorable direction for markets to operate freely, explicitly and effectively.

3.2.1 Ownership

Ownership stipulates property of various assets in economy, especially property of means of production. Ownership shows property form, property scope, property object.

About property form, human history underwent many different social regimes, so there leads to changes in ownership form of assets. In primitive Commune regime, there did not exist individual ownership form but only public ownership, in former Socialist nations there only had collective ownership form and State ownership about means of production and did not accept private ownership about means of production. Nowadays popular existence model in the world is to diversify ownership forms, including: State property, collective property, private property, common shares ownership. Property form diversity leads to economic sectors diversity.

Scale of property is necessarily concerned, it shows which assets and how its scope is possessed by economic sectors. Majority of current countries do not limit scale of assets property; class of assets, which is right to possess, is relatively diversified from land, company to financial tools.

Ownership objects often include external and internal sectors. However, each country has various regulations about ownership participation rate of external and internal sectors. For example, in current Vietnam, external investors are not allowed to hold over 49% share of each internal common enterprise, particularly bank is not allowed over 30%.

Ownership means important in market economy. It stipulates assets ownership legally, so it helps economic subject self-control in business operation, motivating economic development.

3.2.2 Business operation scale

Business operation scale of enterprises has a relatively great difference among countries. In countries with developed market economy, business scale is more broadened in comparison with newly converted countries into market economy model. In assistance in America you can open casino but in Vietnam can not. Business scale also depends much on social political regime at each country. Especially business lines are related to communication information, publishing, press or artistic culture.

3.2.3 Equality rate among economic sectors

Each country has many economic sectors in same existence and development: Public sector, collective sector, public company sector, small and mediate enterprise sector, household sector and external investment sector. Market mechanism requires equality among economic sectors who all participate in common playground. This is equality among public and private sectors, among external and internal economy sectors. The equality shows business scale, capital accessibility, land accessibility. Basically, nations all have more priority to domestic economy sectors compared with external investment sectors, if different, it is only at priority. For example: In Vietnam, from January 01st, 2009 commodity distribution market has newly opened for external investors, formerly from April 01st, 2008 foreign bank has just been opened bank subsidiary at home, while sectors have been developed by organizations for a long time. In developed countries, internal big enterprises capture from foreign partners must be accepted by Government or legislatures of home country.

3.2.4 Administrative interference in economic management.

Basically, administrative interference in economic management is in contrast to market economy principle. However, such administrative interference with benefit or harm for that country also depends on its specific situation. Control of exchange rate or limitation of capital flow out of or into a nation is expressions of administrative interference, but it has a benefit for market economy newly converted nations, or nations short of economic management experience. As can show that, continuously changed tax policy is another form of administrative interference, such this makes difficult for forecast about enterprises' business operation plan. Sub-permit barriers established by intermediate managers cause a great obstacle for business operations and common operation of market.

On the other hand, admission is also that market economy itself sometimes makes mistake and can cause a serious consequence. Therefore, in some cases, administrative interference at suitable level can be necessary. For example when happening to commodity supply shock, market situation becomes confused due to monopolization in aleatory operation, then market control aiming at to master aleatory influences is considered to necessary to stabilize market.

3.3 Fiscal year policy

Fiscal year policy of Government includes tax policy and annual expenditure plan.

3.3.1 Tax policy

Each nation has distinct tax policy, showing at tax flows, tax type and tax rate for each kind. Tax is main revenue source of State policy and used to sponsor for many regular expenses by Government. Tax policy is often decided by legislatures at each country and it can change, but slowly due to ratification of many levels.

There are two main tax flows: direct tax and indirect tax. Direct tax includes personal income tax and enterprise income tax. Personal income tax includes all items from salary, bonus to revenue by investment operations. Personal income tax is applied for persons with income from some level over and often calculated under accumulation system. Enterprise income tax is not calculated under accumulation but only the same tax rate, this tax imposes on enterprise's profit. Beside the two types of tax, social insurance can be also considered another type of direct tax.

Indirect tax includes one type as: value-added tax, special sales tax, import and export duty and assets tax. Value- added tax is applied for business operation enterprises; this tax is calculated on accrued value of enterprise made goods. Special sales tax is imposed on commodities and services which society does not (not yet) encourage to use, for example: sales tax of tobacco, beer and alcohol, etc cruiser or event auto. Import and export duty is applied for goods and services dutiable when these goods are sold in external countries (export) or bought from external ones (import). Assets tax is applied for individuals who hold a lot of valuable assets as real estate, heritage, and antiquities.

Tax policy and economic yield

In this part, we survey tax policy influence on total supply, demand of domestic commodity and finally decide economic yield. Figure 3.1 shows model of total supply and demand in short-term time (1 year) of economy. If there is not any considerable change influencing production and consumption, two lines DD and SS are defined as total demand and supply lines of domestic commodity in the next year time. These two lines meet at the point G correlatively with yield Q_0 and average rate P_0.

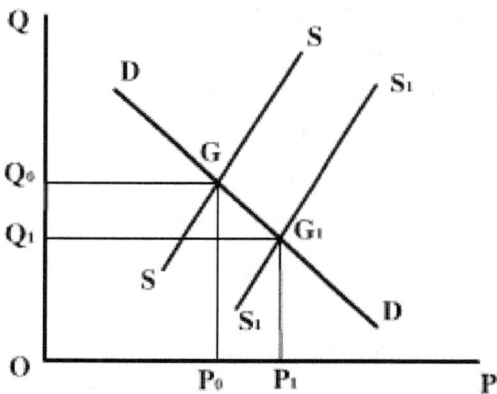

Figure 3.1: Change in short-term equilibrium state when Government increases value added tax

Now it supposes that all other elements of economy do not change, and particularly tax policy changes, namely Government decides to increase value added tax. When increased tax raises general expense of all commodity and services, this leads to influencing business operation. Total supply line SS will be gradually shifted to the right of diagram at new position S_1S_1. Value added vat increase does not affect short-term total demand on line DD. Two lines DD and S_1S_1 meet at the point G_1 correlatively with yield $Q_1 < Q_0$ and rate $P_1 > P_0$. Hence increase in value

Market Economy & Policy On Two Domestic Currencies

added vat raises goods and reduce economic yield.

With the same economic background above, if Government preserves value added tax, instead of that increase enterprise income tax, demand - supply situation also changes the same, and it finally leads to reducing yield and increasing price.

Consider in contrary case, if Government does not raise tax but reduces tax, then business operation condition of enterprises will be more favorable. Therefore line SS, instead of shifting to the right, will shift to the left and cut line DD at a position correlatively with higher yield and lower price.

If Government does not change taxes related to enterprise's business operation but changes personal income tax, our concern is to move from total supply to total demand. For instance, Government reduces personal income tax rate strongly, this makes available income of families increase. Then, total demand line DD shifts strongly to the right at new position D_2D_2 as shown at figure 3.2.

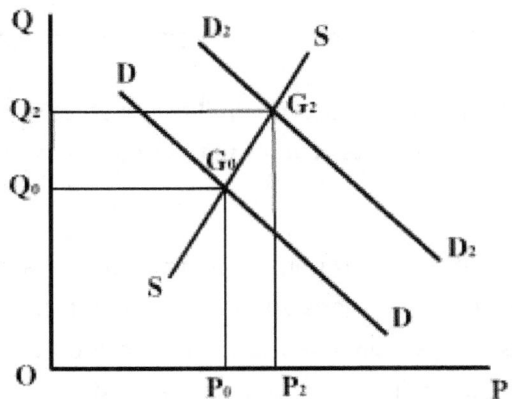

Figure 3.2: Change in short-term equilibrium state when Government reduces personal income tax

Change in personal income tax does not have a direct effect on business operation of enterprise block, so that total supply line SS still preserves. Two lines SS and D_2D_2 meet at the point G_2 correlatively with rate $P_2 > P_0$ and yield $Q_2 > Q_0$. In case personal income tax does not reduce but increases, total demand line shifts to the left to establish equilibrium position at lower rate and yield reduces.

Import and export duty also influences total supply and demand of domestic commodity and so it changes economic yield rate. If Government decreases sharply import duty of lots of commodities and services, that will influence total demand and supply for domestic goods - services, when all other elements preserves,

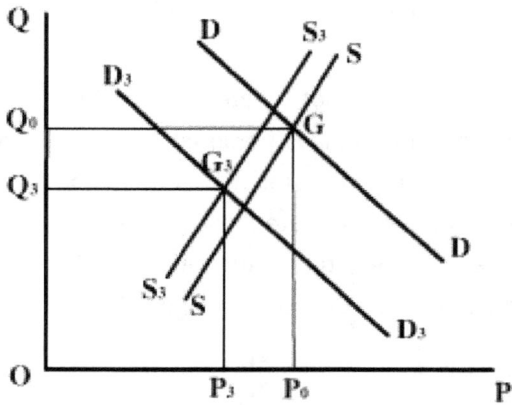

Figure 3.3: Change in short-term equilibrium state when Government reduces commodity import tax

As for business operation, due to lots of abatement import materials, expense of business operation has a little bit decrease and hence it shifts total supply line from initial position of SS to new one of S_3S_3 at figure 3.3. As for demand, because of strong abatement import goods, so demand of internal goods reduces obviously, at that time total demand line of internal goods shifts from DD to new position D_3D_3. New total supply and demand lines meet at the point G_3, correlatively with yield $Q_3 < Q_0$ and rate $P_3 < P_0$. If do the opposite, not decrease tax but increases commodity income tax, total demand – supply line will shift in the opposite direction compared with the above part and establish yield and price rate higher than before.

If preserve import duty but increase sharply service – commodity import tax, it also has a bad effect on domestic production. At that time, import and export commodity will meet difficulty because tax expense increases higher compared with former one. Therefore, total commodity supply of domestic production declines, and total supply SS shifts to the right at the position S_4S_4 as figure 3.4.

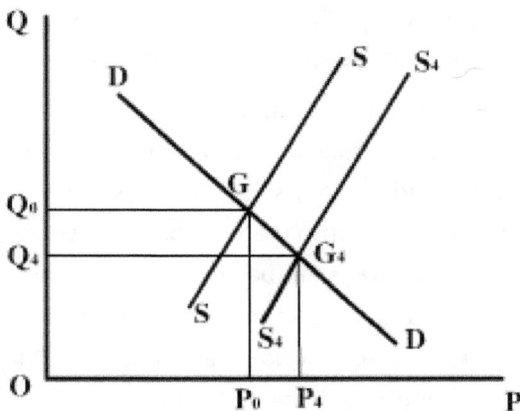

Figure 3.4: Change in short-term balance state when Government Raise commodity export tax

Commodity export tax increases highly that does not influence a demand line, therefore total demand line DD still preserves. Two total demand and supply lines (DD & S_4S_4) cut at the point G_4 correlatively with a price rate $P_4 > P_0$ and yield rate $Q_4 < Q_0$.

Situation will change completely contrarily if import and export duty reduces sharply instead of the sharp increase above.

Practically, some taxes can change together, then we analyze an impact of each tax, afterwards combine to have final model about total supply and demand of domestic commodity, then determine price rate and new equilibrium yield relatively.

3.2.2 Government's expenditure

Government's expenditure can be divided into two parts: basic expenditure and extended expenditure.

Basic expenditure is expenses to remain common operations of machinery of the state and pension scheme, social benefits. It consists of salary and allowance for civil servants, spends regularly on education, medical, security, national defence, pension salary, unemployment benefit and social security. This is the relatively expense every year and it only changes when raising salary and allowance.

Extended expenditure includes accounts invested into basic infrastructure works as bridges and road, harbor, electricity and water; spending deeply on education, scientific researches, medical, security, national defence; investing into material basis for Government agencies. This extended expenditure is annually unstable but depending on actual demand and State budget. In some cases, due to implementing many investment projects, so beside accounts assisted by budget, Government must mobilize capital through bond issue and external borrowing.

Government's expenditure and economic yield

Nowadays over in the world, mostly Governments spend from 1/4 to 1/2 of GDP, this is a rather great ratio. Therefore Government's expenditure plan has a great effect on economic growth at each country. Figure 3.5 describes a change in short-term equilibrium state of each economy when Government has a sharp increase in expenditure compared with initially calculated plan.

Market Economy & Policy On Two Domestic Currencies

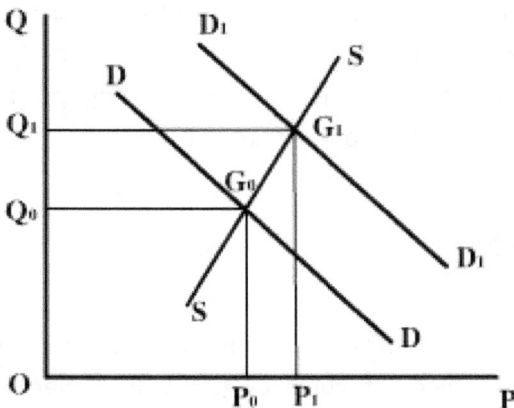

Figure 3.5: Change in short-term equilibrium state when Government increases expenditure

In the normal conditions, total demand line DD cuts total supply one SS at the point G_0 correlatively with average price P_0 and yield rate Q_0. Sharp increase in Government's expenditure shifts total demand line DD to the right at position D_1D_1. Total supply line preserves because of not being influenced by decision on Government's expenditure increase. Two lines SS and D_1D_1 meet at the point of G_1 correlatively with average price $P_1 > P_0$ and yield rate $Q_1 > Q_0$. In contrast, if Government reduces expenditure compared with the initial plan, total demand line will be moved to the left of diagram to establish a new equilibrium state at lower and price rate.

Government's expenditure plan depends on economy's state through basic macroquota as inflation, growth or unemployment. When economy is in good operation, Governments need to limit expenditure to avoid warming up economy, similarly reduce national debt and save resources for use when in need. Otherwise, when yield grows low, unemployment increases and deflates. Government can increase expenditure to encourage economic demand in order to create more jobs and stabilize macroeconomy. To ensure Government's economic demand stimulation with long-term effect, requirement about investment expenditure from policy (or borrowing capital for investment) must bring a high effect, creating positive change in economy and activating private sector.

3.4 Currency policy

In majority of countries, Central Bank is assigned to manage currency policy. Object of currency policy in Government's general objects is to stabilize macroeconomic quotas. Central Bank's basic functions are to issue currency, ensure liquidity for economy, control activity safety of commercial banking system, and stabilize price and economic yield.

3.4.1 Tools of currency policy

Currency market is economy's life-line; it includes interbank market, credit market and foreign exchange market. Central Bank controls currency market through currency policy. To implement currency policy, central Bank is often used some "useful tools" as compulsory reserve ratio, discount interest, credit limit and open-market operation aiming at to affect currency market.

Compulsory reserve ratio

Commercial banking system is functional to mobilize capital and implement a loan for all economic sectors. Because commercial banks are allowed to release payment cheque in replacement for cash use, from amount of certain cash, they can make bigger amount of money than many times. For profit target, commercial banks can borrow at maximum rate. To ensure liquidity and safety of credit activity, Central bank stipulates compulsory reserve ratio about cash at commercial banks. Compulsory reserve ratio is minimum ratio reserve cash in total mobilized amount at each bank. In necessary cases, Commercial bank can change the reserve ratio at commercial banks, hence it changes total amount of paid money (M1) in economy

Discount rate

Commercial banks must reserve amount of compulsory cash under central Bank's regulation. But in case customers draw more cash than commercial bank's anticipated values, that makes amount of reserve cash deficit, at that time commercial bank must reborrow on interbank market or from central Bank to make up for deficit reserves. Interest rate which central Bank lends commercial bank in short-term time is called discount rate. By setting discount rate, central Bank can influence interbank interest and from there it is cash reserves rate at commercial banks. When discount rate increases higher than average interest on free market, commercial banks need to be careful in lending and raising cash reserves to prevent shortage of compulsory reserves.

Credit limit

Credit limit is a quota which central Bank applies for commercial banks to prevent the phenomenon running after profits, and then it leads to lending at random and losing system security. Credit limit of total banking system depends on economic growth speed and expected inflation rate. Credit limit of particular bank also depends on administrative ability and risk control quality in its operation history.

Open market operation

When in need of changing amount of cash in economy, central Bank undertakes transactions on financial market by purchasing or selling out amount of certain securities. It assumes he want to increase more currency supply of one hundred billion, central Bank buys amount of bond of one hundred billion on securities market. Then bond reserves of central Bank increase up to one hundred billion and economy has more

100 billion of cash into circulation. When in need of reducing currency supply in economy, central Bank sells reserves securities to collect money.

Through currency - financial markets, central Bank can also influence foreign exchange rate of domestic currency in comparison with other foreign currencies. To reduce domestic currency rate, central Bank must use domestic currency to buy foreign currency on the free market for reserves, then foreign currency becomes scarce and raises price in comparison with domestic currency. In contrast, to raise domestic currency rate, central Bank sell reserves foreign currency out to market to collect domestic currency.

3.4.2 Currency policy on money appreciation

We rewrite exchange equilibrium equation which has studied at former chapters:

$$PQ = MV$$

P is average price rate of all goods – services (called commodity)

Q is total quantity of transaction goods paid

M is total par value of circulated currency (M1)

V is a number of average circulations of currency unit

From the above equation we can take out formula M: $M = \dfrac{PQ}{V}$

With common economic conditions, V can change in short term but little change if in consideration in mediate or long term time (from 1 year over). When M, P, Q change, we have formula as follows:

$$(M + \Delta M) = \dfrac{(P + \Delta P)(Q + \Delta Q)}{V}$$

$$= \dfrac{PQ + \Delta P.Q + P.\Delta Q + \Delta P.\Delta Q}{V}$$

$$\rightarrow (M + \Delta M) = \dfrac{PQ}{V} + \dfrac{\Delta P.Q + P.\Delta Q + \Delta P.\Delta Q}{V}$$

Because $\dfrac{PQ}{V} = M \rightarrow \Delta M = \dfrac{\Delta P.Q + P.\Delta Q + \Delta P.\Delta Q}{V}$

Call g is economic growth rate, p is inflation rate, m is money increase rate M1, we have: $\Delta M = m.M$, $\Delta P = p.P$, $\Delta Q = g.Q$,

$\rightarrow m.M = \dfrac{p.PQ + g.PQ + g.p.PQ}{V} = \dfrac{(p + g + pg)PQ}{V}$

$= (p + g + pg) \dfrac{PQ}{V} = (p + g + pg)M$

$\rightarrow m = (p + g + pg)$

Because p, g are small values (about some percents), p and g are relatively small in comparison with (p + g), for this reason, m ≈ (p + g).

$(M + \Delta M) = \dfrac{(P + \Delta P)(Q + \Delta Q)}{V}$

$= \dfrac{PQ + \Delta P.Q + P.\Delta Q + \Delta P.\Delta Q}{V}$

$\rightarrow (M + \Delta M) = \dfrac{PQ}{V} + \dfrac{\Delta P.Q + P.\Delta Q + \Delta P.\Delta Q}{V}$

$V \times \dfrac{PQ}{V} = M \rightarrow \Delta M = \dfrac{\Delta P.Q + P.\Delta Q + \Delta P.\Delta Q}{V}$

Like this increase rate of M1 is equal with total inflation and economic growth rate. Hence central Bank can be through a control of M1 to master inflation and economic growth.

Short-term interest on currency market

When central Bank chooses currency policy in direction of appreciating total means of payment (M1), market interest will change under demand of money in economy. Figure 3.6 is currency market model, horizontal axis shows nominal quantity of money and vertical axis is nominal interest on currency market.

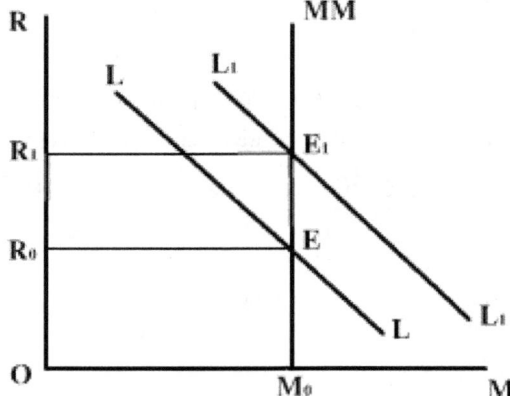

Figure 3.6: Short-term equilibrium state on the currency market when money supply is fixed

LL is economy's demand line of money in short-term time correlatively with yield rate in advance. Along line LL, when nominal interest rate increases, demand of money reduces. MM is nominal supply line of money, when money supply is fixed, line MM is upright at money supply rate of M_0. Two lines LL and MM meet at the point of E, correlatively with interest rate of R_0 on currency market.

It assumes since some advantageous elements make economic yield more increased than expected, and then money demand line LL will move to the right of diagram at the position of L_1L_1 as on the figure. Because money supply is fixed, two lines L_1L_1 and MM cut at the point of E_1 equivalent with interest $R_1 > R_0$.

3.4.3 Currency policy on interest appreciation

Currency policy on interest appreciation originates from the opinion which is said that if interest rate, which fluctuates too largely in comparison with inflation rate is not good for economy. P_0 assumes to be basic inflation rate expected for the next time, if nominal interest rate is much larger in comparison with p_0, depositors are profitable

Market Economy & Policy On Two Domestic Currencies

while business operation objects meet difficulty. In contrast if nominal interest is smaller than p_0, depositors are unprofitable and enterprises will enjoy profit. Hence, if the lowest interest rate on the currency market is equal with basic inflation rate, it seems to harmonize profit among them.

When central Bank chooses currency policy on interest appreciation, they do not master amount of currency but at that time demand of money will decide amount of money supply. Central Bark assumes to choose basic interest at R_0 (R_0 is equal to basic inflation rate expected for the next time). If interest on currency market is bigger than R_0, Central Bank is ready to raise money supply so that interest gradually reduces at R_0. In contrast, if market interest is smaller than R_0, central Bank tries to collect money so that market interest gradually shifts to at R_0.

Volume of money for supply in short-term time

Figure 3.7 is an equilibrium model on currency market when central Bank fixes interest rate at R_0. RR is the fixed interest line through R_0. LL is money demand line about of economy in short-term time equivalent with the yield rate in advance. Two lines LL and RR cut at the point E are defined equilibrium demand rate at M_0.

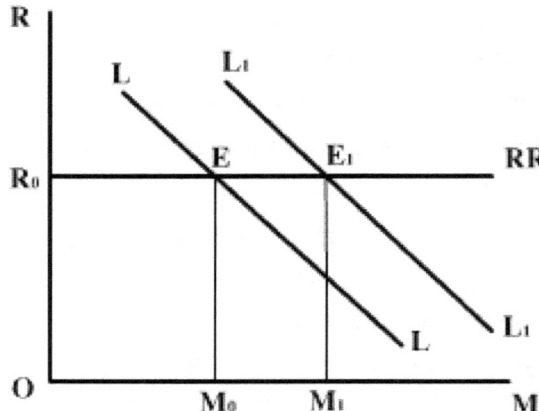

Figure 3.7: Short-term equilibrium state on currency market when interest rate is fixed

It assumes there are reasons making economic yield increase higher than expected, and then the demand line LL shifts to the right at position L_1L_1 **as** shown on the figure. Fixed interest line RR still preserves. Two lines RR and L_1L_1 meet at the point of E_1 equivalent with new equilibrium supply of $M_1 > M_0$.

3.5 Target of macroeconomic regulation

Target of macroeconomic regulation aims at to optimize basic macroeconomic quotas of economy including: economic growth rate, inflation rate, unemployment, and payment balance. In this part we will study about relationship among basic macroeconomic quotas when economy changes, from there we can establish common index which reflects health of economy.

3.5.1 Relationship among inflation, unemployment, economic growth and payment balance

Basic macroeconomic quotas are not quantities which exist independently in economy but in fact they are closed each other. Knowledge of relationship between basic macroeconomic quotas helps us develop suitable target in macroeconomic regulation.

Inflation, unemployment and growth

We all desire that both unemployment and inflation are low, and the higher growth increases, the better it is but that, indeed is very difficult, economists show that, basically there is not any inflation accompanied with low unemployment but must have an exchange between those quotas. To have a low unemployment rate, we need to accept high inflation and vice versa.

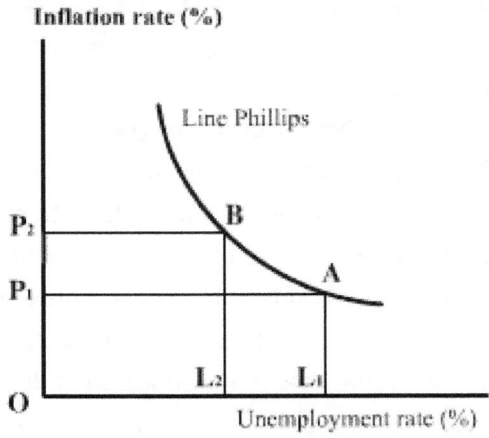

Figure 3.8: Short- term Line Phillips

Line Phillips as on the figure 3.8 describes relationship between inflation and unemployment in short term. Economy currently assumes to be equivalent with position A on the line Phillips, so unemployment rate is at level L1 and inflation rate is P1. When realizing that unemployment is at high rate and it can cause imperativeness for the people, Government will relax currency policy and expand expenditure to stimulate demand for economy. Increase in total demand will raise goods price and services. Because labor salary is slow to change, in the short term increase in price raises enterprise's profits. Therefore, enterprises want to recruit more labor force to expand business aiming at to raise more profits, as a result unemployment rate goes down. Economy shifts from position of A to position B on the line Phillips, then unemployment rate is L2<L1 and inflation rate is P2>P1. Besides, increase in total demand helps raise yield, so Government's policy on demand stimulation increases economic yield, reduces unemployment but raises inflation.

Short term is like this, but in consideration of long term the situation will be different. When inflation rises, sooner or later interest also increases. Similarly salary must be also adjusted to ensure actual salary for laborers. Increase in interest and salary raises enterprises' business operation expenditure, it leads to reducing profits. Economy's scale only increases in the short term, and then temporarily stops at higher rate in comparison with before. Up to now Government's policy on demand stimulation achieves proposed targets as unemployment reduction and increase in economic yield. However, Government's expenditure expansion must still extend more time to remain high total demand correlatively with total raised supply. Until Government's policy stimulation ends but economy does not a new motivation to self-step, yield will decline regularly, unemployment recurs and inflation goes down. At that time economy has risk of opposite shift compared with before; it means to shift from point B to point A on the line Phillips. On the contrary, when ending demand stimulation stage, if economy has more new motivation to develop but not needing assistance from Government, economic yield continues to remain at high rate with low unemployment and relatively high inflation according to Government's demand encouragement target.

Thus, to increase yield and reduce unemployment, Government is free to loosen currency and extend fiscal year policy at random, doesn't he? That can not be allowed because it must depend on current inflation rate, if the inflation is at high rate but Government continues to stimulate economic demand stimulation, it can lead to risk of ineffectiveness. When the inflation is pushed up too high, there will be a strong impact on people's lives and cause trouble at business operation zone. Psychographics and short-term investment activities in combination with speculation will sway market that makes economy become confused, event chaotic. In that background, both yield and unemployment are not improved and inflation is at too high rate. A part from watching for inflation, stimulating demand too many times will cause budget deficit and increase national debt. Therefore, economic demand stimulation must depend on each specific situation, similarly dosage of demand stimulation must be properly calculated not to cause side effect on economy.

Elements affect payment balance

Beside inflation, unemployment and yield growth, payment balance is one of basic macroeconomic quota. In four quotas, three quotas have been considered at the former chapter, particularly payment balance is not mentioned, and so we need study more in this item.

Each nation's payment balance reflects money flow into and out from that country under all forms, by any currency which, in the time of one year is accounted under the conservational currency.

Payment balance is aggregated by three compositions including: trade balance, current transfer payment and financial balance. Trade balance and current transfer balance are constituted a current balance.

Trade balance reflects services - goods import and export value of each nation. Goods export is called tangible trade (green product, steel, aircraft, etc), services import and export are called intangible trade (tourism, bank, software, etc).

Current transfer balance includes in – out items related to investment profit transfer, dividend, insurance, allowance, aid, oversea national currency exchange.

Each country's financial balance reflects in – out items, not discriminating circulation currency, related to indirect and direct investment activities of all economic compositions – including Governmental investment.

If one nation's payment balance > 0, we have surplus in payment balance; if payment balance < 0, it is a deficit in payment balance; if payment balance = 0, we have square payment balance.

Each nation has deficit in payment balance; it shows that total influxed money is smaller than outfluxed money. If that situation lengthens, it will reduce strongly domestic investment resources and decrease national reserves. Payment balance is an indicator about each nation's investment absorption in comparison with the rest over in the world, or in other words, it expresses its competitive capacity in the international aspect. Two basic compositions of payment balance are trade balance and financial balance. All effort of each nation aiming at to improve trade balance and absorb more external investment flow contributes to beatify payment balance. Each nation with stable politics situation, complete market economics system, abundant human resources will be favorable for attracting international investment flow. Dynamic economy, with reasonable inflation quotas, balanced investment and consumption, steady growth, high competition, trade balance can be a surplus.

When one country is in deficit of payment balance, its domestic currency will be weak in foreign exchange market. Decrease in domestic currency rate is advantageous for export and limits import, helping improve payment balance to some extent. Government can reduce payment balance deficit by currency relaxation aiming at to collapse domestic currency but it will cause a pressure on inflation.

3.5.2 Target of macroeconomic regulation

Target of macroeconomic regulation is to try to optimize basic macroeconomic quotas of economy. Namely, growth rate is high, low inflation, unemployment is low and payment balance is residual. But because macro quota is closely related to each other in favorable direction or unfavorable direction, each economy's requirement must accept exchange among those quantities.

Designate g is growth rate of GDP, p is inflation rate, l is unemployment rate, and t is % conversion payment balance rate of GDP under %

Of the above quotas, we desire g and t to increase, and p and l to reduce. Therefore, if we set $\frac{g+t}{p+l}$ = k, the bigger value of k is, the better it is. **k is called general macroeconomic index** of economy.

Now we try to assign specific data to calculate value of k. One nation assumes to have growth rate GDP at 7%, inflation rate at 5%, unemployment rate at 6%. Payment balance equivalent with 5% GDP.

We have: g = 7%, t = 5%, p = 5%, l = 6%. → k = $\frac{g+t}{p+l} = \frac{7+5}{5+6} = \frac{12}{11} =$ 1.09 = 109%

For other example, if g = 8%, t = -1%, p = 8%, l = 5%. → k = $\frac{g+t}{p+l} = \frac{8-1}{8+5} = \frac{7}{13}$ = 0,5384 = 53.84%

Consequently after all, target of macroeconomic regulation is to try to increase the value of general macroeconomic index k, while k = $\frac{g+t}{p+l}$

We altogether answer one macro econometric closed with reality as follows: It assumes one nation is growing with macroeconomic quotas which are anticipated for the next year: growth rate of 6%, inflation rate of 5%, unemployment rate of 8%, and payment balance at equilibrium state. Let's regulate economy to increase macroeconomic index.

Firstly, let's calculate general macroeconomic index k as initially anticipated as follows:

$$k = \frac{g+t}{p+l} = \frac{6+0}{5+8} = \frac{6}{13} = 0.4615 = 46.15\%$$

We realize that unemployment rate at 8% is relatively high while unemployment rate at 5% is relatively modest when in comparison with unemployment. Growth rate at 6% is not considered high growth, while unemployment is at 8% shows that part of labor force is lost. Payment balance is anticipated at balanced rate it is not too bad. Target of macroeconomic regulation in this case is to reduce unemployment, raise yield, accept higher inflation rate, and payment balance tries to get at rate ≥ 0.

It assumes Government does not have many effective investment projects, so there is not any demand of more bond issue to extend expenditure, so it only concentrates on currency policy. We choose a solution of currency relaxation to stimulate economy. When investing more amount of money in circulation, market's initial reaction is that interest has a tendency to reducing. Interest reduces that increases investment and consumption, therefore goods price will increase chronologically. Increase in price raises profit of enterprises and so it will stimulate them to broaden production and finally to create jobs for economy. Currency relaxation is at proper rate so that how inflation rate increases and stops at 8% at the end of year. Much ability with such policy will reduce unemployment rate from 8% down to 6,5%, and expected growth rate from 6% up to 7,5%. When increase in inflation will reduce domestic exchange rate if other nations have lower inflation, but let's assume that other nations also have solutions to increasing their economy's competition. Therefore trade balance is considered not to change in comparison with initial expectation, i.e., it is at the equilibrium rate.

In summary, we have: growth rate at 7,5%, unemployment rate at 6,5%, inflation rate at 8%, payment balance is at equilibrium rate. Let's recalculate general macroeconomic index k:

$$k = \frac{g+t}{p+l} = \frac{7,5+0}{8+6,5} = \frac{7,5}{14,5} = 0,5172 = 51,72\%$$

Firstly, before having adjustment plan, macroeconomic index expected: k = 46.15%. After implementing regulation policy of economy, we have k = 51.72%. Comparing these two numbers, we realize 46.15% < 51.72%. Hence macroeconomic regulation brings better result.

3.6 Macroeconomic regulation under the first resolution group

Nowadays, mostly countries apply mixed economy mechanism, on the one hand creating a good condition for free market to operate effectively and self-regulate, on the other hand Government is ready to use macro regulation tools to adjust economy when realizing it has a sign deviating from equilibrium orbit.

Policies on macroeconomic regulation are nowadays popular based on the basic principles that market economy itself is able to self-regulate effectively and Government should only interfere in economy at limited rate or interfere in when it meets obstacles. To implement this regulation scheme, the first requirement is to improve market economics system and combination in currency – fiscal year policy. Macroeconomic regulation under the first resolution group has three notes as follows:

1. Create all good conditions for market economy to operate effectively.

2. Implement currency policy in direction of interest appreciation

3. Fiscal year policy brings inaction, depending on private economic sector.

First of all mechanically, legislative machine regularly updates information, supplements lacks to improve economics system in direction of creating a favorable condition for markets to operate effectively, reduce verbose administrative procedures in order to enhance business operation, build a fresh competitive environment, prevent monopoly and commercial fraud.

The second matter is to implement flexible currency policy and always to follow market. Central Bank appreciates high interest tool use to impact economy and not pay much attention to amount of currency. Depending on macroeconomic quotas' development as inflation, unemployment, and current yield together with future expectations, central Bank defines basic interest rate on currency market. To ensure that interest platform turn around basic interest, central Bank adjusts quantity of circulated currency in economy through business activities. If market interest platform is higher than basic interest, central Bank will increase money supply for economy, if actual interest is lower than basic interest, central Bank will collect money. For central Bank, inflation control seems to more prior, so basic inflation rate often has a strong effect on decision on interest. Basic interest rate in equality with basic inflation rate can be an proper choice.

The third matter is fiscal year policy which is considered insurance solution for economy. When economy is in tendency to hot development Government can raise tax or reduce quota to reduce fever for economy. If unfortunately economy falls in recession, Government will reduce tax aiming at to support business operation and raise expenditure for demand stimulation. Government's expenditures are considered a counterpoise for private economic sector aiming at to equilibrate the overall economy.

Policy on macroeconomic regulation under this direction has relatively simply characteristic. The Governments restrict maximum of administrative interference in free market to avoid deforming economy subjectively, the Government appreciates market mechanism highly and regards as an economic motivation. In currency policy, central Bank defines interest and relax quantity of currency, it can be considered to be very clear, creating liquidity in economy and vesting for commercial banking system.

However, macroeconomic regulation policy according to this solution has lots of defects. First of all, it expresses passive, because it is based on market mechanism appreciation and only adjusts economy when happening breakdown, so this solution follows market and tries to solve the consequence caused by market. While market mechanism sometimes makes a mistake, not including objective exterior impacts which deforms market. In currency policy, central Bank vests their self-control high for commercial banking system, but this system does not operate completely and control risk well at any time. Sometimes, because of profit, some banks can lend below standard with big quantity so that it turns into bad debt which causes unsafety for system. The financial crisis originated from lending under its standard in America, now it changes into globally economic crisis but not know when it ends, whether it is a warning bell for currency control relaxation or not. Once having pursued economic policy under this solution, fiscal year policy is in inaction. Governmental expenditure activity is not stable but periodical, it increases strongly when economy depresses and reduces violently when economy develops warmly.

3.7 Macroeconomic regulation under the second solution

As we know market mechanism is basically good, but conceals much risk, so we can not rely absolutely on it. Policy on macroeconomic stabilization under this solution has big adjustments in comparison with the first solution pointed out as above, with three outstanding features:

1. Implement market management through management of some basic markets.

2. In currency policy where the currency control is appreciated

3. Fiscal year policy seems initiative and relatively settled every year.

To implement macrocosmic regulation under this solution, firstly

Governments must rely on basic macroeconomic quotas of former year together with expectations for the next year to make a plan for economic development for the whole year. This plan must be also included objective impacts from the world beyond and domestic consumption investment psychology. The fiscal year policy is made available and reflected in nation's overall economic development plan in the next year. The final key is that policy making organs must point out anticipated basic macroeconomic quotas for the next year as: growth rate, inflation rate, unemployment rate and payment balance. If in the next year, there is not a big fluctuation inland and in the world impacting estimated basic quotas, macroeconomic management for the overall year will follow close behind those quotas.

3.7.1 Market management through management of some basic markets.

There are many objective and subjective reasons impacting market economy and deforming demand and supply relation. Any Government can not anticipate objective shocks risen from natural calamity, epidemic diseases or war. But there are lots of social elements which have a strong impact on market change such as overproduction, psychographics under movement, and investment under a crowd or aleatory operation. Therefore, Governments is required to have suitable solutions to manage market aiming at to avoid subjective elements which thrust market economy into danger.

But if too worried about market fluctuation, officials control closely all development on market, it can cause a great costliness and injure for economy. Because close management deforms market mechanism, annuls business motivation and its acquired result is a slack economy. Hence, the core matter pointed out is to have method of proper market management to both get management target and little cause damage to market mechanism.

We realize that in market economy, goods groups have a mutual relation. If rice price increases, it will raise price of other cereals and also increase price of cereals – made products, increase in petroleum will impact series of items. When real estate market is eventful, it brings about development of related lines as: building materials, interior, construction. Credit market increases warmly, it proves that there are too many enterprises dedicated to investment and it can conceal the next risks. When real estate price or share price increases strongly, it will raise assets price of almost the public and it can activate high increasing demand of consumption. Because of the mutual impact between markets in economy, if we manage some basic markets well, we can control the whole markets indirectly.

Three important markets, which we must pay attention to, are: credit market, real estate market, and securities market.

Credit market combines closely with consumption and investment activities in economy. Those are essential services of banking activity and having an effect on system's safety. Therefore, we need to manage this market in credit growth and service quality.

Real estate market has a big capitalization, each household or each enterprise owns or rents real estate. Real estate value and market's development rate have much effect on economy, so the management is necessary.

Securities market is especially meaningful in economy. This is the long-term capital mobilization channel for enterprises and where it attracts external and domestic investment capital. Securities market makes a contribution to converting common enterprises into general public joint stock company model which is managed and controlled better. Securities market management should focus on information transparency about types of posting goods, control market scale and enhance transaction activity control.

Credit market

Credit market's center is a commercial banking system and a

financial organization with credit activity function. Around this center block is a grouping of household and economic organization that has a demand of lending and borrowing capital. Banking system is only an intermediary bridge to transfer capital from redundant place into short one in the whole economy. Basically, amount of credit is directly proportional to scale of economy. When the higher economy growth increases, the bigger demand of credit is. Because the inflation devalues currency, total nominal credit value also increases together with inflation rate. Thus if there is not any change, total annual credit rate is equal with total economic growth rate and inflation rate.

If call d rate of amount of annual credit, g is economic growth rate, p is inflation rate, so we have: $d \approx g + p$.

In fact, enterprises can mobilize capital through other channels as: company bond issue or share issue on securities market. Therefore, total amount of annual credit can change depending on eventful level on securities market. In the period when securities market becomes exciting, enterprises will issue bigger amount of capital and reduce credit funding. And when securities market slopes down, amount of capital mobilization through securities channel declines strongly, the enterprises return to traditional credit channel. Therefore, value of d is unnecessarily equal with (g+p) at any year.

We can divide credit funding objects into main groups: investment credit and consumption credit. Investment credit includes enterprises' loans to deploy new investment projects or expand their business operation. Consumption credit is consumption loan for households and individuals with demand. Depending on inflation state's development, sometimes central Bank needs to control all consumption loans to contribute to demand and supply equilibrium in the whole economy.

In normal conditions, total annually accrued investment of economy also rises with rate equal with total economic growth rate and inflation rate. One nation's total investment includes elements: private sector's investment, mobilized capital from securities market, direct investment, Governmental investment and bank credit investment. Hence, central

Bank needs to base itself on economy's actual development we can hope to bring out suitable credit rate for commercial banking system.

Real estate market

Formerly, when economic condition is difficult, the demand of accommodation, dressing is considered to be urgent. At that time, labor productivity is low; all resources of society only concentrate on assisting the urgent demand but not yet. Nowadays, the situation has been changing basically, wealth in society increases many times, labor productivity raises high, and goods are very various. In majority of nations, the demand of accommodation, dressing is essentially met, event these demands are ranked on equal term with series of the others in a modern society as: telephone, internet, music, film, tourism, drug, etc.

Real estate market includes main parts as: dwelling and land for people, office for lease, industrial land. Demand of real estates completely depends on real situation of country's economy. The higher income of each citizen is, demand of dwelling also increases, the more economy develops the bigger demand of office and industrial land is. Therefore in consideration of a long term, growth speed of real estate market is equal with economic growth speed. If in a short term, real estate market increases warmly, irrevocably it will decline strongly later.

When in comparison with other goods market, we realize that real estate market has smaller aperture, it means goods on the market only consumes inland but there is not any export of real estate products. Real estate supply has much bind related to land scheme and depending on natural land area of each nation. Value of real estate is relatively difficult to define since there is a regular change of scheme and conversion of land use purpose. These elements create a favorable condition for aleatory operation on real estate market

Real estate has large capitalization and it impacts many other markets, heat – cold of real estate market also causes difficulties for other relevant business operation sectors. If know that, basically and long real estate's growth rate is equal to economic growth rate, why do not we manage this market but continue to bear its unusual fever?

To manage real estate, we need to care about price fluctuation and growth rate of the whole sector. Real estate price increases quickly that will raise household's assets price and can cause strong consumption effect that leads to rising inflation. Annually average growth rate of real estate value equal to basic inflation rate is rational. The best annually average growth rate is equal to economic growth rate. However, due to people's emigration process from rural area to urban one, each local's growth rate in each country is different. To manage real estate market well, we need to improve relevant law regulations as: register procedure, transaction, real estate tax. Besides, construction statistics at locals needs to be carefully controlled, we can know growth situation of real estate sector exactly.

Once land agency defines growth rate of annual real estate sector equal to economic rate, when realizing appearance of its fever, we need to apply management measures, for instance reduce credit related to real estate or pause real estate projects invested by the State. In contrast, when real estate's growth rate rises more slowly than economic growth rate, we must have market encouragement policy, including State budget use to raise social housing fund.

Securities market

Common joint - stock company is the company organization model which is considered the most advance today. From world leading groups in technology area (Microsoft, Intel, IBM...), or giant oil firm (BP, Exxon mobil...), even great bank groups (HSBS, Citigroup, etc), all are common joint stock enterprises. Securities market gives strength, brings up the most advanced form of enterprise today and continues to create a good condition to multiply this model.

Securities market includes two markets: Share market and bond market. Share market is long-term capital mobilization channel for enterprises, its collected capital through share issue becomes enterprises' ownership capital, and it is different from the capital from bond issue or credit borrowing. Bond market is medium-term mobilization channel for enterprises and even Government, its collected capital from bond issue is time-limit capital from themselves investors but not through intermediary organizations as lending bank. For economy, capital mobilization through securities market is less risk in comparison with bank capital. Because enterprises mobilize directly on the securities market from investors, if enterprises work at a loss afterwards it only influences one group of investors. And in case enterprises borrow capital through bank but works at a quantity loss and not pay debt, it will be a risk of impact on the whole banking system.

Due to being posted a bill and transaction on securities market, all information about enterprises is manifested, their final business result reflects on share price. Enterprises do business roaring, share price raises high that profits for investors and enterprises trades ineffectively, then share price goes down and it can make shareholders lose. This causes enterprises excited and makes a contribution to enhancing competition for the whole economy.

However, beside its advantages, we need to add securities market limitations. In securities market, bond market is less risk, and share market conceals much risk for investors and economy. When share price increases high, despite of firm increase or illusive raise, investors' assets which are converted into money also rises quickly. Therefore, they can accelerate expenditure and self-reward them valuable items which reflect the success in their investment result. If many people do the same, it is clear to contribute to increasing inflation in economy. When share price slopes down, investors' expenditures are also deducted and even lots of investors do not stand hopeless shocks of securities market.

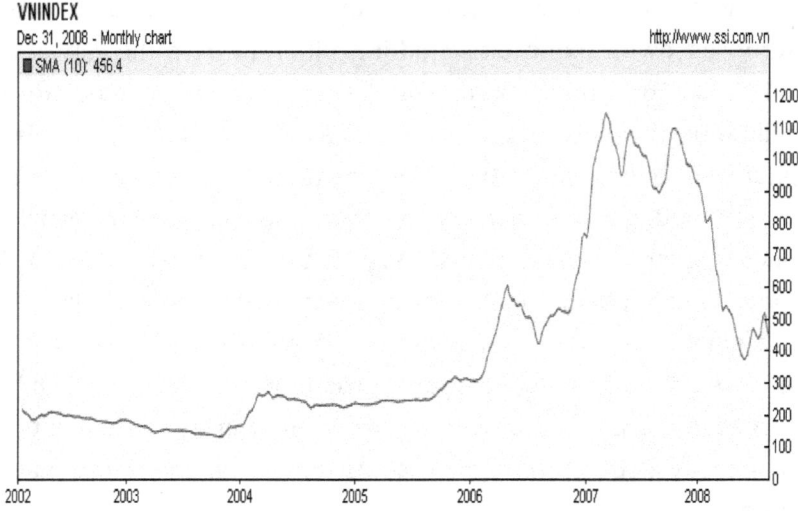

Figure 3.9: Fluctuation of VN-INDEX from 2002 to 2008. Source www.ssi.com.vn

Figure 3.9 is chart of VN-INDEX in the stage from 2002 to 2008. This index was relatively settled in the years from 2002 to 2005 and boomed in 2007 then sloped down in the year 2008. Figure 3.10 is chart of DOW JONE in the stage from 2009 to 2008. Particularly in year 2008 index of DJIA seized nearly 40% and returned at rate of six former years.

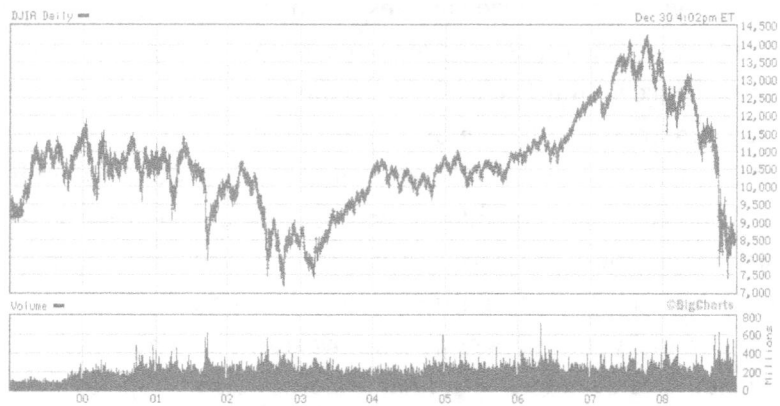

Figure 3.10: Fluctuation of DOW JONE from 1999 to 2008. Source www.cnn.com

Due to insecurity of securities market, its management is necessary to limit risk for market and economy. Market's scale should be proper with economy's one and investment flow's quality. Economy's scale is defined through some quotas as: sum of posting securities, sum of posting quantity and sum of market's capitalization. Investment flow's quality shows short and long term investment purpose and investor's qualification. When investment flow is mainly medium or long – term, similarly almost investors have a deep knowledge of securities market they can broaden market's scale. In contrast, if investment flow into securities market is mainly short-term, concurrently investors participate in form of movement, participating in securities is main; we must restrict market scale to avoid bad consequence later.

Share price on securities market depends on domestic macroeconomic situation and business operation as well as each enterprise's long-term development strategy. Therefore, State management agencies need to strengthen to declare periodically macroeconomic information, and posting enterprises must manifest information to help investors evaluate potentiality of each type of securities. State Securities Commission needs to improve market supervision from enterprise's information declaration, or securities issue to services related to consultancy, securities transaction to ensure market to operate equally and effectively.

3.7.2 Currency policy

Macroeconomic regulation under the second solution is considered a careful solution. Currency policy is run in direction of currency appreciation. Rate of total means of payment M1 is equal to total economic growth rate and expected inflation rate. At the time of ending of the year, Governments all have the basic macroeconomic quotas of the former year in their hand as: inflation rate, unemployment rate, economic growth rate and payment balance. Based on quotas of the former year together with macroeconomic forecasting for the next year, national policy making organs can give proposal to Government about macroeconomic quotas for the next year. National budget can be based on Government's macroeconomic management plan for the next year to determine currency supply for economy, so that rate of total means of payment M1 is equal to economic growth rate and expected inflation rate. After having determined currency supply rate for the next year, Central Bank implements money supplement into circulation regularly every month in the whole year.

Once central Bank controls total means of payment, its interest on the market will self-regulate to equilibrium state. If at any time average interest on currency market is much bigger in comparison with actually basic inflation rate, maybe because people expected higher inflation rate compared with practice. Only little time later, when practically basic inflation rate is declared, savings deposits will raise and demand of capital will reduce, then interest rate declines little by little to set up new equilibrium state. Interest on the market will have a tendency to equilibrium at equal rate with actually basic inflation.

It assumes that central Bank implemented regular currency supply and total means of payment M1 increases firmly from time to time then interest on the currency market still balances at too low or high rate in comparison with practically basic inflation rate, its cause may not belong to currency policy. There were other causes that made economy fall in too cold or hot state. Then we need to reconsider management work on the basic market or must adjust fiscal year policy.

3.7.3 Fiscal year policy

Fiscal year policy in the second solution means active, it is set up before giving basic macroeconomic quotas under the plan. Fiscal year policies include Government's tax policy and expenditure. If there are not external and domestic elements which cause a macroeconomic fluctuation, the fiscal year policy enforces in conformation to the

Market Economy & Policy On Two Domestic Currencies

proposed plan at initial time.

It proposes fiscal year, currency policy and basic markets regulation take place according to Government's anticipation, but there are several signs showing that some macroquotas indicate weak, for instance growth rate is low and inflation rate is lower in comparison with expected. Then fiscal year policy which is a necessary element must adjust firstly. Government can issue more bonds to attract capital from society and strengthen investment in projects more effectively aiming at to raise total demand for economy, create more jobs, restore economic yield. In contrary case, if economy grows higher than anticipated enclosed with high inflation, Government needs to cut down really unnecessary projects promptly to reduce total demand and finally to decline fever for economy.

Chapter 4
POLICY ON TWO DOMESTIC CURRENCIES

Market economy is still considered a currency economy. Any economic activity, despite of being small or big also is closed to currency use. The more market economy develops, the bigger monetary – financial market scale is. Financial tools are usually created to meet an investment demand of various objects. Transaction volume in the actual economy possesses smaller rate in total currency transaction volume of the whole economy.

In process of world economy integration, parallel with international commercial outbreak, capital flow also turns over quickly, regularly and with bigger volume among nations. These links leading indispensable result is to depend mutually among nations and territories more and more increasingly. Therefore, shocks of supply and demand in actual economy or shocks on the financial market can take place more regularly and influence reciprocally under chain reaction which increases inertia degree of inflations in economic cycles.

All those issues make more complex for economic situation in each country and cause a great pressure to Governments in macroeconomic operation. In lots of cases, decisions on currency policy show less effectively that makes "patient" more and more dangerous. **Policy on two domestic currencies** is designed to aim at contributing to a resistance increase of actual economy before the more monetary – financial market pressure is broadened in the scale but the more risk, insecurity it conceals.

4.1 Currency circulation flow in economy

Figure 4.1 shows five various market groups of the whole economy. Participants in markets are called set A, including families, all enterprises under different fields of economy and including State Administrative bodies. Commodity production enterprises, commercial companies, securities companies, gold business companies, commercial banks, hospitals, etc, individuals and households all are under Set A. Collecting all markets which is called Set B, divided into five market groups including:

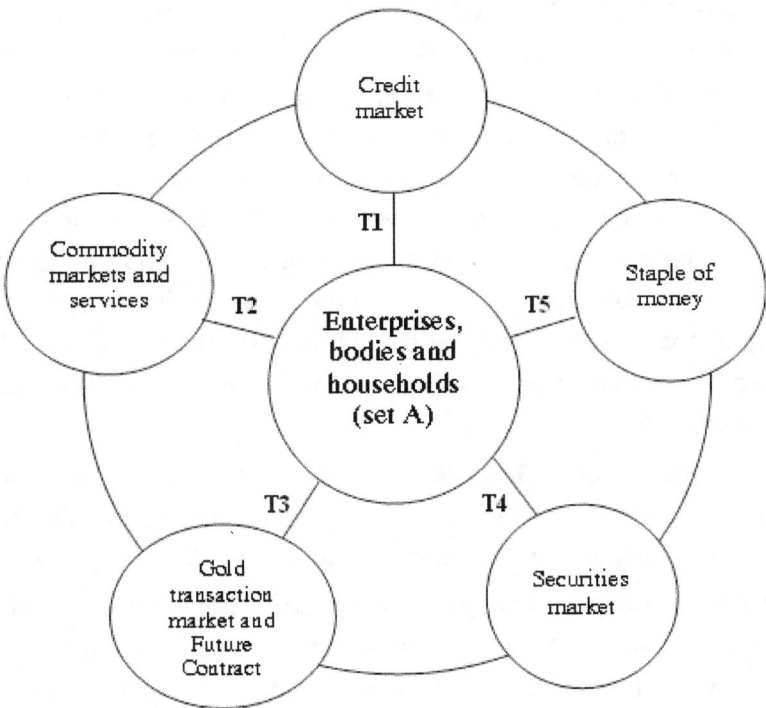

Figure 4.1: Various market groups of the economy

Market group 1 - Credit market: Centers of credit market are commercial bank system and financial organizations which provide credit service. Customers of this market include many objects from individual, household to enterprises; they have a demand of consigning savings or funding from bank.

Market Group 2 - Commodity market and normal transaction: Group 2 has very large scale, consisting of all commodity and service markets which serve production and consumption in economy. For example: food market, real estate market, steel market fuel market, educational service market, labor market. Consumption households and business production businessman are the familiar consumers of the market group 2. Besides, other objects under set A also participate in market group 2 at some level.

Market group 3 - Gold transaction market (precious metal in general) and future contract. Gold trading floor and future contract trading floor are Centers of market group 3. At these trading floors, commodity is not dealt as at normal goods markets but only paid on investor's transaction account. In our country, there have just been some gold trading floors and not ever been any future contract trading floor; but in developed countries, future contract and gold trading floors are very popular. Customers of market group 3 are individuals or organizations; they buy and sell continuously on their account to look for profit, not like commodity sale for production or consumption at market group 2.

* ***Market group 4 - Securities market.*** Securities market consists of bond market and share market. Participants in securities market include Securities Companies, organization investors and individuals.

****Market group 5 - Foreign currency market***: Securities market is a site taking place exchange activities between domestic and foreign currencies. These market participants comprise: Organizations and individuals who have demand of selling and buying foreign currency to serve production and consumption, investors, organizations and individual of foreign currency operation.

Each object under set A can participate in different market groups, for example: one household often buy commodity and service at commodity market. They also join in credit market by sending savings at bank and investing shares on securities market. Commercial banks are centers of credit market but they also participate actively in securities market, currency market and gold transaction market – future goods. Each enterprise has the credit relation at bank. They need to convert foreign currency at group 5 to import and sell goods – services on market group 2.

4.1.1 Compositions of total means of payment

Participants in market must have one of two things: goods or currency for transaction. Overall consideration is that monetary flow and community flow always equilibrate valuably. At each market group there are always commodity quantity and currency quantity which lie in wait to prepare for transaction process in the next time. Entrepreneurs all have reserve goods to serve customers wherever, whenever; households often save amount of money for daily expenditure; banks must reserve amount of cash to ensure payment, investors also reserve money in account and take advantage of occasion to show off.

Calling T_1, T_2, T_3, T_4, T_5 respectively provisions to serve transaction at five market groups. At any time, each currency is owned by and used for a certain purpose, so it must depend on one of five above provisions. T_1 is the reserve for credit market activity; therefore T_1 is reserved in commercial banking system and credit agencies. $T_1 = M - M_0$, while M is the total issued cash outside central Bank, M_0 is cash in circulation. We see that in all transactions at four market groups, from market group 2 to market group 5, paid currency is cash or giro cheque. Hence total means of payment M_1 is equal to total transacted reserve outside banking system: $M_1 = T_2 + T_3 + T_4 + T_5$.

4.1.2 Speculation and investment trend deforms markets

Business objects in all economic fields can be divided into two groups: investors and speculators. Any composition, despite of individual or organization, when joining in business operation process is for profit. But speculator and investor's method to look for profit is different. Investors deal under law of value; it means when cheap, they buy and when expensive, they sell. For market investors, the market sometimes makes a mistake, when too hot or too cold. Speculators deal relied on short-term signal of market, they sell based on psychology of majority, not conform to law of value. In speculators' eyes, the market is always correct, even when it is too hot or too cold. At any such market, there are always two compositions: investor and speculator, but if investors predominate, market's development is often stable and trades more effectively. In contrast, at the market in which speculation overwhelms, it is a very high risk and can lead to market crisis.

It assumes the market group 2 has inflation, and then total demand of goods is bigger than the total supply that makes price increase. If bank interest is low and profit at investment channel under groups 3, 4, 5 is unsatisfactory, venture capital flow maybe transfers from four remaining groups to market group 2 which makes currency T2 suddenly increased. Strong increase in T2 will rise goods price and push inflation rate higher. This bad situation can be only improved if central Bank interferes by cutting down money from circulation and rising basic interest. In fact, there often happen securities shocks or gold shock, then speculation flows from everywhere flock in the market where there are shocks and turns it into assets' blister which can blows up at any time.

4.1.3 Market fevers' affect on macroeconomic situation

Like this speculation and investment trend changes reserves under market group 5. Currency is concentrated on the market group happening to a fever and reduces at less eventful market group. Now we consider market fever's impact on macroeconomic situation in two correlative cases with two choices in currency policy are: currency policy on money appreciation and currency policy on interest appreciation.

Market fevers' affect on macroeconomic situation in case central Bank implements currency policy on money appreciation.

It supposes interest is initially at low rate, volume of means of payment is fixed, when psychographics raises that increases commodity price at market group 2. If profit rate at other investment channels is unsatisfactory then venture monetary flow flocks in market group 2 and makes T suddenly increased. Good price continues to increase and goods yield also raises. T2 increases since venture capital flow from market groups 3, 4, 5 into T1 is nearly stable. Hence at the first stage of goods price fever, bank interest rises. Then inflation comes on to rise as a result it will push bank interest higher. Because central Bank pursues policy on currency stabilization, saving interest can not increase quickly and it follows inflation. It is a good condition for aleatory operation at market group 2 to continue increasing. When investment flow flocks into market group 2, assets price at other markets reduces sharply and becomes attractive. Investment flow starts to leave market group 2 to move into other safer investment channels. Goods price can not continue to accelerate but will increase slowly, so distance between interest and inflation ratio narrows. Until interest rate is equal or bigger than inflation ratio, speculation phenomenon begins to decrease violently. At the end of fever cycle, goods price and interest all are at high rate.

When speculation flow leaves goods market at group 2, goods price returns to go down. Capital can flows strongly into credit market that makes interest reduce. This is the period when goods price does not raise, and interest also continues to reduce gradually to a low rate. Economy moves to a flat stage with low inflation, low yield and unemployment will increase. Hence this speculation flow creates cold – hot fever on goods market, making a contribution to forming business operation cycle and impacting strongly macroeconomic quota.

Market fevers' affect to macroeconomy in case central Bank implements currency policy on interest appreciation.

It supposes interest rate at first is low and central Bank is ready to supply currency volume to satisfy all demand of economy. Different from the above part, a fever here assumes to begin from commodity market group 2 but come from securities market. Venture capital flows from other markets alternately crowd in securities markets to search for profits. Securities index starts to increase gradually and causes investors excited. Due to low interest rate, capital source from credit channel moves to securities market relatively much and commercial banks must add reserve sources by borrowing money from central Bank. Share price continuously increases along with fact money flow is flown into higher and higher, but that does not impact inflation and economic yield. Some careful investors withdraw capital from security market and leave playground for later speculators. High increase in share price also raises assets value of part of the people and they strengthen expenditure, excite to go shopping. Now securities market's fever starts in actual economy. Commodity Price begins to increase together with share price's fever. Inflation is a risk of increase and central Bank starts to copy with by increasing basic interest. The next period including inflation, interest rate and securities index go up; at that time economic yield increases and unemployment is low. When inflation and interest rate increase highly, securities index gains the top and starts to go down. Capital flow is withdrawn from the security market and poured into economical channel to enjoy higher interest rate. Although reserves in banking system increase strongly, basic interest rate reduces because central Bank still continues to prevent inflation increase. Hence central Bank tries to withdraw currency in circulation to maintain high interest rate and prevent inflation. Currency volume reduces, share ratio goes down, interest is at high rate, and commodity price can not continuously increase, early reaches the top and goes down. Hot increase in period of economy ends and the next is the gloomy period with high unemployment state and low yield together with inflation reduction.

4.2 Policy on two currencies

Above part we recognize currency flow moving freely among market groups forms unusually cold and hot fever that causes insecurity for economy. In case of any way, the best way is that we should follow natural mechanism which but not administrative orders, we can prevent or restrict market fevers, then economy shall develops more firmly.

In above described market groups, beside credit market, commodity market group 2 and currency transaction market vary little but securities and gold transaction market and Future contract often fluctuate more strongly. Because securities value or gold value are difficult to determine and depend too much on climate elements, economic situation, investment psychology, etc, political issues, such values go up and down irregularly. At market in which goods value is only relative, venture activities take place more popularly and have much risk for economy.

We observe that in market group 2 average price of commodity which fluctuates at 100% per year, is considered to be serious. Even though in developed countries, average price of commodity which varies at 5% per year, also threatens macroeconomic stabilization. While share index or gold price sometimes increases or reduces at 20% every month or 10% each week that is considered to be normal. Note that capitalization level of share market can be equal to GDP, Therefore, we can imagine the big change level of value of assets volume. That arouses the thought: if all service and commodity market groups use one currency in common as a measure of value, there will certainly conceal a risk for economy.

4.2.1 Three economic sectors and two currencies.

It assumes economy uses two different currencies, one currency is signed M_c and another is signed M_i, M_c is main domestic currency and used popularly at normal service and commodity market (market group 2). M_c is also domestic currency used to exchange in foreign currency market (market group 5). M_i is used to exchange in securities market (market group 4) and gold transaction market and future contract (market group 3). Particularly credit market executes to borrow and lend for both M_c and M_i. Figure 4.2 sums up sectors which are commonly used each currency.

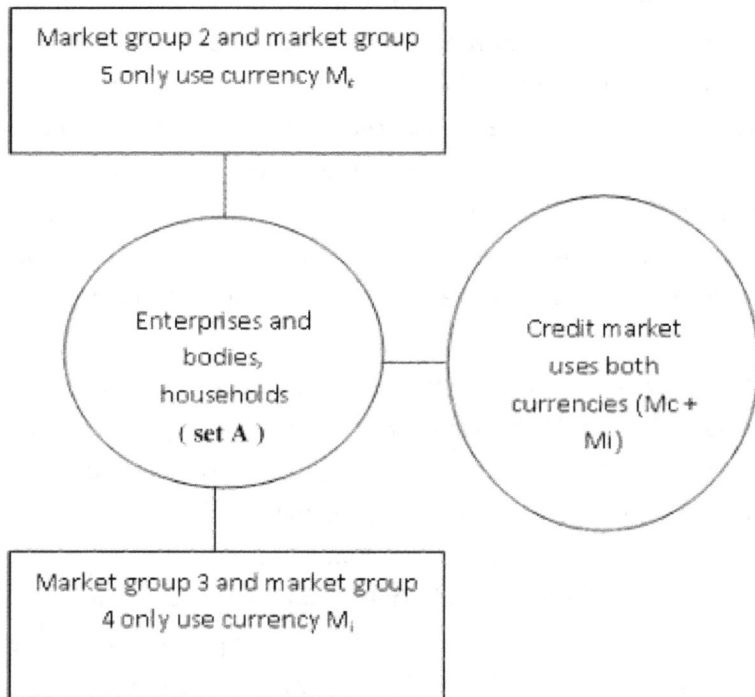

Figure 4.2: three sectors of economy and two currencies

When dealing normal commodity, all objects under set A are compulsory to use currency M_c, and when joining in securities transaction or gold trading floor they only use currency M_i. Two currencies M_c and M_i have the same unit, for example: Viet Nam uses by **dong**, America uses by **Dollar**, and in European area currency common is **Euro**. Two currencies M_c and M_i can be exchanged in banking system according to fixed ratio 1:1 (1 currency unit M_c = 1 unit of currency M_i). Reading till here someone can think, two currencies M_c and M_i have the same currency unit but are exchanged parity, whether they are different or not! But that thought is incorrect. In fact two currencies are very different, only when studying the whole chapter we recognize preeminence of two - domestic currency policy.

Currency issue

Central Bank is the sole organ which issues two domestic currencies. Currency M_c is present currency of each country; it consists of many different face values in convenience for transaction in commodity market. In our country, present currency comprises different face values from 200 **dong** to 500.000 **dong**. Currency M_i has newly issued, it needs some characteristics to differ from currency M_c, but its unit is still calculated the same, Vietnam's currency is called Dong. Since currency M_i is only transacted on the market group 3 and group 4, where payment process is made through account, it is unnecessary to issue lots of face values; even only issue a single face value. For instance in Vietnam, we only issue M_i with its face value of one million (1000.000 dong). Issue of M_1 with such big face value is to differ from M_c, we both save the issue and not also meet difference in payment because currency M_1 is mainly paid on transaction account. After central Bank issues more M_i, then all cash balances on investor's account at market groups 3 and 4 have to be converted into M_i in conformation to regulation, and obviously Central Bank has to draw amount of correlative currency M_c on the market.

Function of two currencies

First of all, both two currencies are convention as a measure of value in commodity transaction on relevant market and both of them all are means of payment. Currency M_c is used at market group 2 and exchanged on foreign exchange market. Daily commodity transaction activities of households or enterprises' business operation all are used by currency M_c. If you have a demand of foreign exchange to travel abroad, you can use currency M_c to exchange; enterprises need foreign exchange to export and they also do the same. Currency M_i is used at market group 3 and group 4. When participating in transaction at these markets, each member is individual or organization who must open transaction account. Money in transaction account must be M_i, if you only have M_c, you need to change it into M_i to use on these markets. When there is a demand of transaction on these markets group 3 and group 4 no longer, you can draw M_i and convert it into M_c to use on other goods markets.

We give some examples for currency transaction between two currencies. You assume to have one hundred million of M_c and you want to convert them into share investment at market group 4. Then Securities Company (or payment authorization bank) will convert one hundred million of M_c into M_i and transfer into your share transaction account. It assumes face value of M_i only has one type of one million dong, your one hundred million is correlative with one hundred folio one million M_i If your initially invested money must not be one hundred million round but is one hundred. million two hundred thousand dong, the exchange from M_o into M_i still takes place the same and your account still has cash balance of one hundred million two hundred thousand of M_i, although amount of money can not convert into round figure with face value of one million by M_i, but it is not important. After exchanging such currency between you and securities company (or payment authorization bank), securities company's cash account is also changed, namely quantity of M_i increases more one hundred million two hundred thousand and M_i will reduces correlatively with one hundred million two hundred thousand dong. Process of share sale on the market, Securities Company on the market will make clearing by M_i on your transaction account according to value of sale items to each currency unit (dong). Hence in your share transaction account, cash balance M_i is odd number according to each unit but not million round.

Market Economy & Policy On Two Domestic Currencies

Until the some time, after many transaction times, in your account cash balance it assumes to be 10.250.000 dong (ten million two hundred and fifty thousand dong), you want to draw that amount for other uses, you can receive ten million of M_i (correlative with ten folio one million dong M_i) plus 250 thousand by M_o (this amount is due to conversion from 250 thousand M_i into M_o at securities company) or you can convert the whole currency of M_i in the account into 10,250,000 dong by M_c at securities company. Hence we see that although currency M_i only has one face value but not cause difficulty in payment on the market groups 3 and 4.

To be convenient for currency management, objects under set A are not absolutely used in replacement with currencies M_o and M_i for payment. If any object purposefully uses two currencies in the way "take the wrong sow by the ear", he will bear strong penalty, even may be seized money.

Both two currencies can be used for value reserve as present types of currency. Commercial banks and credit organizations all implement to borrow and lend both M_o and M_i, they are allowed to issue payment cheque for both currencies but when making clearing for customers, they irrevocably comply with principle for each type of currency in transaction.

Bond and share issue.

On the bond, share market or gold trading floor, means of payment is used by M_i. These markets all are secondary, commodities are properties bought and sold many times. The issuing market is called primary market, where share or bond is issued at the first time, later it is posted transaction at the secondary market. At primary market, firstly issued securities are conversed its values by M_c, investors who buy more issued or firstly issued securities all are convention by M_c. Dividend or bond interest on the shares which an organization issues to pay for an investor is also by M_c. Currency M_c is also used to pay due bond. Only at secondary markets, all transactions are only calculated by M_1. Use of two currencies at two primary and secondary markets has its reason. Actually there are many investors buying share or bond to hold for a long term and not to participate in transaction on the secondary market, so convention of M_c as face value for the firstly issued bonds is reasonable. Moreover, objects of bond or share issue all are for money collection to serve their business operation, so payment by M_c by investors is more convenient.

4.2.2 Exchange rate between two currencies.

All participants in investment on the market group 3 and group 4 must be used by M_i, if at present they only have currency M_c, it is compulsory for them to convert into M_i for transaction. In contrast, when moving the area of business from market group 3 and group 4 into the others, they must convert from M_i into M_o. Hence, demand of conversion among two currencies is very large and expresses constant for investors. In underdeveloped countries, markets under group 3 and group 4 have a relatively modest scale, but in developed countries, capitalization rate of share or bond market can be bigger than GDP and daily transaction value is very high. Investments include many compositions: Individual, enterprise, economic organization, internal and external investment fund. Their investment is also very various, depending on economic capacity, not limiting the highest or lowest rate. Therefore, the most essential requirement is that conversion among two currencies must be convenient, easy; it can take place at bank, Securities Company, brokerage firm at gold trading floor or at future contract trading floor.

Exchange rate between two currencies is the essential matter of two – domestic currency policy. That rate irrevocably is 1:1. There are many reasons to see that two currencies need to be exchanged parity. **First of all**, two currencies have the same calculation unit (for instance Vietnam's currency all is called ***dong***) but exchange is not parity that is difficult to accept. **Secondly**, share, bond indexes or commodity price indexes on markets group 3 and group 4 are calculated by M_i ; if currency M_i is no parity with currency M_c we must establish one more index calculated under M_c so that other objects are convenient to monitor - thus it will be very complicated. **Thirdly,** if two currencies are not exchanged parity there will appear domestic currency trade, like foreign currency which causes more trouble for economy.

To ensure exchange rate between two currencies M_c and M_i is 1:1, central Bank' currency control plays an important role. Central Bank can consider M_c a main currency and adjust value of M_i under M_c. With exchange rate agreed by two currencies is always 1:1, if realizing a demand of M_i increase central Bank needs to raise demand of M_i in the market, inversely central Bank cuts down M_i from the market. It is easy to implement these solutions through open market business.

The fact shows that demand of investment and speculation in markets group 3 and group 4 is insecure but changes relatively strongly according to time. When share market becomes eventful a demand of investment increases highly, then amount of money from other sectors flocks into securities market. After share price reaches the top and goes down, invested capital quickly leaves securities market to find a place to reside safely. General commodity markets often do so, in case business operation condition is favorable, a demand of investment increases and in inverse case, amount of invested capital reduces strongly. Because amount of money in circulation between two sectors of use of M_c and M_i is insecure, central Bank is required to be very flexible in new currency control to ensure that parity exchange rate between two currencies takes place swimmingly.

4.2.3 Currency policy in economy where there is a use of two currencies

Figure 4.3 describes the groups which use each type of money in common and reserves for payment are correlative with each market group. T2 and T5 are reserves by currency M_c to implement transaction on on the markets group 2 and group 5. T3 and T4 are reserves by M_i to perform transaction on the markets group 3 and group 4. T1c and T1i respectively are reserves by M_c and M_i at commercial banking system and credit agencies.

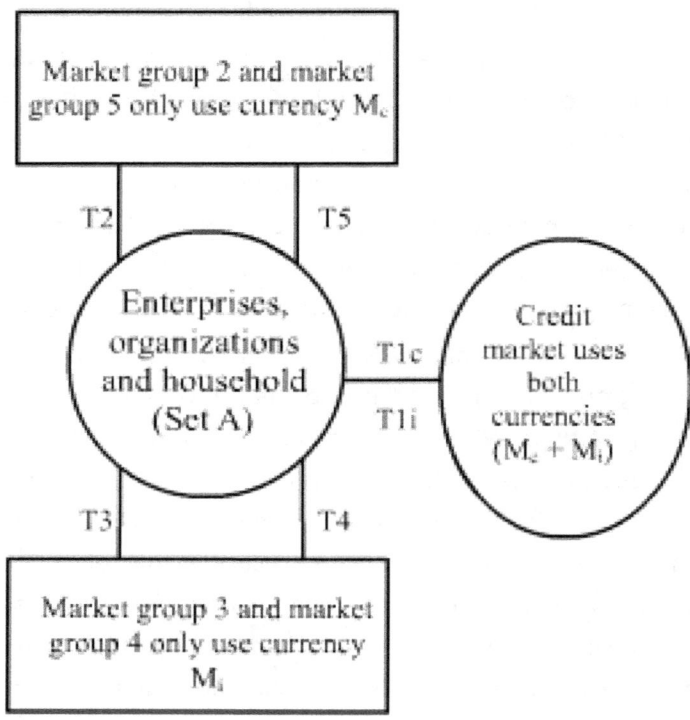

Figure 4.3: Transaction reserves are correlative with each currency at three sectors of economy

Amount of cash and total means of payment

If we call Mc total value of cash by M_c issued by central Bank, Mi is total value of cash by M_i issued by central Bank. Then total value of cash is calculated by both currencies M = Mc + Mi issued by central Bank

Designate M0c and M0i in turn are total value of cash of currency M_c and M_i in circulation outside commercial banking system & credit agencies, we have:

$$M0c = Mc - T1c \; ; \; M0i = Mi - T1i$$

In the economy in which it only uses one currency, total means of payment is signed as M1. It is equal with paid reserves at four market groups from group 2 to group 5: $M1 = T2 + T3 + T4 + T5$.

With economy in which it uses two domestic currencies, total means of payment in the whole economy is equal with total two quantities of means of payment correlative with two currencies. If call M1c total means of payment by M_c and M1i is total means of payment by M_i, we have: $M1 = M1c + M1i$.

Outside commercial banking system and credit agencies, M_c is transacted at the market group 2 and group 5, M_i is transacted at the market group 3 and group 4. So we have: $M1c = T2 + T5$; $M1i = T3 + T4$.

Policy on currency control

Basic target of currency policy is to control inflation and contributes macroeconomic stabilization. In economy in which it uses two currencies, economy's basic activities are only related to M_c. And currency M_i is only transacted on the market group 3 and group 4 so it does not influence directly inflation or economic yield. The focus of currency policy in economy in which there is a use of two currencies concentrating on control M_c.

Total means of payment in circulation by M_c is $M1c = T2 + T5$. If foreign exchange transaction market is improved into a centralized market and professional foreign exchange business objects have to open transaction account there central Bank can control reserve of M_c at centralized foreign exchange market as they are controlling reserve cash at commercial banking system. When there is centralized foreign exchange market, reserves of M_c there will be correlative with amount of T5 which is reserving to transact foreign exchange on currently decentralized market.

Through commercial banking system, central Bank can control M1c.

Through centralized foreign exchange market, central Bank can control T5. Hence central Bank will control T2 because T2 = M1c − T5.

Exchange equilibrium equation has a form: PQ = MV → P = MV/Q. In this equation quantity V/Q little changes so P and M fluctuate in the same direction. Applying this equation for market group 2, M is exactly equal to T2. Therefore, if central Bank completely controls T2, it will control average price rate (P) at market group 2, i.e., control inflation situation.

Hence in economy in which there is a use of two domestic currencies, main currency M_c is transacted in a narrower scope in comparison with the case economy only uses one domestic currency. At markets group 2 and group 5, the goods price as well as exchange rate often fluctuate lightly so policy on currency operation should be in direction of currency appreciation for main currency M_c. Namely, amount of M_c is properly increased with economic speed of growth and expected inflation level.

Once currency policy attaches special importance to currency control, interest of M_c is decided by market. Since in this case M_c is only transacted in narrow scope, it has little element impacting interest of M_c. Hence interest of M_c will move flexibly and follow close behind actual economy's development; it will be more rational and contributes to regulating economy better in comparison with the case economy only uses one currency.

In economy where there is a use of two currencies, M_c is the main currency and M_i is secondary currency. Currency policy applied for two currencies will be different. For M_i, central Bank only focuses on control under principle of ensuring parity exchange rate between two currencies. Volume of means of payment is by M_i, much or little amount is not important, but the more importance is to stabilize exchange ratio 1:1 between two currencies. Central Bank only needs to control total means of payment by M_c and parity exchange ratio between both currencies is also relaxed for total means of payment by M_i.

Special cases

Any economy has a risk of depressing or falling into crisis due to objective reasons. The economy which uses two currencies, can also apply currency and financial policies to stimulate economy as the economy only uses one currency as currently. In such situation Government actively regulates amount of M_c in circulation in favorable direction for the economy. Amount of M_i at that time needs to be adjusted on to ensure parity exchange ratio between two currencies.

4.2.4. Speculation's affect in economy where there is a use of two currencies

We have considered impact of speculation and investment trend to the economy where there is a use of one currency and realizing those activities deform markets and are the important reasons causing economic insecurity. In market where it is used two currencies, there still exists speculation activities but scale is smaller and has a less impact on economy.

It assumes increase in psychographics intensifies service and commodity prices on market group 2. Increase in price helps profit of business operation sector become more attractive. Then short-term capital flow and speculation everywhere is directed toward the market group 2. But let's note that, to do business in market group 2, investors or speculators must have capital by currency M_c. Beside market group 2, there has market group 5 and currency M_c using credit market, so a part of capital which has a property of speculation from the credit market and group market 5 also flocks to the market group 2. T2 continues to increase but quickly reaches the top since central Bank tightly controls the total means of payment by currency M_c. Commodity price level also rises according to increase level of volume of T2 and shall stop increasing when T2 reaches the top. Interest rate by M_c at first increases slowly but later it does faster than commodity price speed and this contributes to preventing commodity fever on the market group 2. It is because in this case, the fever on the market group 2 quickly is put down since: on the one hand, central Bank controls the total means of payment by currency M_c, On the other hand, currency M_c is only used on a narrower scale, so scale of venture capital is also smaller.

As above we have just mentioned short-term investment flow and internal shifting speculation in the common use sector of currency M_c but not taken notice of investment flow from market group 3 and 4 that probably flows into market group 2. To participate in business on market group 2, investors on markets group 3 and group 4 must convert M_i into M_c. So when having a fever on market group 2, demand of currency M_c raises suddenly but demand of currency M_i decreases strongly. To ensure parity exchange principles between two currencies is not broken down; central Bank shall sell major volume of bonds to decrease quantity of M_i in circulation. Since supply increases strongly price of posting bond by M_i goes down and become relatively attractive for the long-term investors. Notice that, face value of bond and dividend is calculated by currency M_c so when price of posting bond according to currency M_i decreases strongly investors under sector of currency M_c also jump into securities market to hold cheap bond. They need to convert M_c into M_i they are just allowed to participate in securities market. Hence speculators in markets group 3 and 4 want to convert currency M_i into currency M_c, in contrast bond investors in sector of currency M_c need to convert M_c into M_i, consequently demand is automatically equilibrated. Any amount of invested and venture capital in use sector of currency M_i is converted into market group 2, that amount of invested capital in common use sector of currency M_c is converted into the securities market. Besides, when price of bond reduces strongly credit interest in commercial banking system becomes less attractive and is pushed up higher, so more and more it quickly it contributes to reducing goods market group 2.

We continuously consider impacts of securities fever to the actual economy. It assumes there is an inner reason that makes share price strongly increasing. Short-term investors and speculators flock to share market. Among them, many objects in sector of currency M_c also want to change into share market. So demand of M_i increases high, to stabilize exchange ratio 1:1 between two currencies, central Bank must increase supply of M_i by buying major amount of bond in securities market. Since demand of bond highly increases that makes the posting price of bond by currency M_i increasing. Some Investor can buy bond to get money for share investment. Many careful investors can also sell bond and share with high price to add capital for business in sector of currency M_c. Demand of conversion between two currencies M_c and M_i of investors is automatically equilibrated. When price of share and bond increases many investors get profits and assets of a part of the people go up and they bravely spend on shopping. Till to now influence of securities fever starts to spread out to area of actual economy. Increase in total demand in area of market group 2 leads to making commodity and service price. Inflation will quickly increase interest rate. When interest rate rises at some level securities fever will stop. Total demand in area of group 2 gradually stabilizes and so price level stops at stable rate, inflation gradually reduces. Finally interest rate little by little decreases and return at equal rate with the interest one of the stage before securities fever happens.

In the above examples we recognize price fevers which come at any market, finally impact market group 2 and influence to actual market. But in economy where it is used two currencies its margin has a smaller effect than in economy where it is used one currency. To get that because in the economy where there is a use of two currencies, its transaction scope of main currency M_c is considerably narrowed and central Bank is easy to control to total means of payment by M_c.

4.3 Conclusion

We know, in the economy where there is a use of one domestic currency central Bank often applies currency policy according to two tendencies: Interest appreciation or currency demand control.

Currency policy on interest appreciation increases initiative right for commercial banking system, creating high liquidity and clearness in economy but there conceals much risk before the danger forms assets' blister, bad debt, extraordinary economic cycle.

Currency policy on currency supply control appreciation brings more caution, less risk in the overall aspect but it has affectedness for the economy, sometimes less liquidity and causes inhibition in some markets, especially in financial markets such as securities or maturity transaction.

Policy on two domestic currencies as presented above made the very good advantages strength and restricted disadvantages from the project for two - currency control in economy where there is a use of one currency. Currency supply control for M_c helps actual economy develop stably, and looseness of M_i helps increase liquidity and open up much opportunity for financial market.

If analyze carefully, we can realize two – currency policy brings a better result than the first expectation. Supply control of M_c helps the actual economy stabilize, when actual economy stabilizes the financial market also varies with smaller margin. Once both areas of the economy has high stabilization venture activities go down, invested capital flow overwhelms. Human resources in society is redistributed under more basic direction, profits business production in the areas of actual economy, thence it contributes to increasing competition and improves labor productivity in the whole economy.

Market Economy & Policy On Two Domestic Currencies

www.ingramcontent.com/pod-product-compliance
Lightning Source LLC
Chambersburg PA
CBHW051705170526
45167CB00002B/543